30 Days to a Better Me

30 Days to A Better Me

Consciousness Cleanse & 21 Days of Fitness

Ms Kamesha

30 Days to a Better Me

Copyright © 2016 Ms Kamesha

All rights reserved. No part of this publication may be reproduced, distributed, or transmitted in any form or by any means, including photocopying, recording, or other electronic or mechanical methods, without the prior written permission of the publisher, except in the case of brief quotations embodied in critical reviews and certain other noncommercial uses permitted by copyright law.

Printed in The Unites States
First Printing, 2016
978-0-692-59302-8
Ms Kamesha, LLC
Lithia Springs, Ga 30122
www.mskamesha.com

30 Days to a Better Me

Dedication

This book is dedicated to my son Kenneth Destin McCrary. Each day I look into your eyes, you give me a thousand reasons to be a better me. Mommy loves you!

Acknowledgements

First, I want to thank the man above, because without God none of this would be possible. In May of 2015, I believed in your word, and I step out on faith to follow my dreams. When times get tough, I know that I can depend on you to show me the way. For so many years, I made my plans, not realizing that what you had already planned for me was better than anything I could have imagined, and I just want to thank you for that.

To my miracle baby Destin, thank you for everything. I know you are too young to understand the impact that you have had on my life, but you changed me for the better. I will never forget the day August 1, 2013, I was driving and felt like I had to throw up, and your GG told me to take a pregnancy test. I was in denial because I was told by my doctor's that it was a chance that I wouldn't have children, so I took six pregnancy tests and went to the emergency room because I couldn't believe I was finally pregnant. Ever since that day, my life has changed for the better. I know that you depend on me, and I promise that I will always work hard to make sure you have everything you need and want. Mommy loves you so much, more than life.

To my Mama, where do I start? You have sacrificed your whole life for me to be successful. God had favor on us and a plan for us because we knocked all of the statistics out of the park. You had me three days before your 15th birthday, you were judged, denied the things you loved, and you had to push your dreams aside for me. When I was younger, I didn't understand the struggles that you went through, but now I understand. I cannot thank you enough. You have always believed in me and told me that I should follow my dreams. I know that you are truly my #1 supporter and fan. When I work so hard, and sit at home "thinking" I am not only working hard for myself and Destin but for you too. I want to make you proud, I know that nothing that I do can bring back the time you missed growing up, but I can make you proud, and show you that every struggle that you went through wasn't in vain. Without your love, talks, gifts, and financial help, I do not know where I would be. You make my life easier, and I thank you and love you so much. This book could be about all that you do for me and the sacrifices you have made, but since it's not I have to end this. I know you just smiled, and you are smiling reading this. Love you and I could never thank you enough. Phil, I didn't forget about you! I am truly blessed to have you in my life. You love Destin like your own and me, and you are always there when I need you. You are my #2 fan, and I appreciate you for everything.

To my "Mamalois" God knows I wished you were here with me. I know that you would be happy and proud of me. I am just like you, and I know that my mama and I get our strength from you. The last ten years have been different without you. I always think about you and wished you were here to enjoy all of these precious moments, especially Destin. I know you are looking down on me, and you are with me every step of the way. Without you, I would not be the woman that I am. I was your baby, and you have always loved me, spoiled me and protected me, and I will forever be thankful. R.I.P Mamalois I love you.

To Rodney, you have been there the last ten years of my life, through all of the ups and downs. Together we created my biggest blessing, and I will forever be thankful. I sometimes know you don't always understand my dreams or why I work so hard, but no matter what, you stand right by me. Thank you for stepping up to the plate and doing what a man supposed to do, and allowing me to follow my dreams. One day you will see that all of the late nights on my laptop was worth it. Love you and thanks again.

To Uncle Greg, I am not sure if you are going to read this book, but just in case you do, I want to thank you. You are an example of the man I want my son to be like. You have always pushed me to be the best me. When I had lost focused, I would hate to go around you because I knew you would tell me that I needed to get it together. I never wanted you to be disappointed in me; I have always wanted to make you proud. Thank you for being the example of how a man supposed to be.

To my aunties (Aunt Jeneal, Linda, Jenelle, Sherry, Chitta, and Toni), thank you for always being a support to me. I know that I can always count on you guys to be there for me when I need you. I love you and thank you for loving and believing in me.

To Terrica and Short, thank you guys for everything. We are more like sisters, than best friends. You guys have been my #1 supporters. I haven't had too many special moments without your presence or help. Thanks for being the listening ear and being there when I needed some advice or just to vent. You both teach me so many things, and help make me better, and I love you. It is always a no judgment zone when we talk and are together, and because of you, I know what it feels like to have a friend.

To my family and friends, thank you so much. There are so many people out there that supports me, and I appreciate you all. If I name everyone, this part would be ten pages, but just know I am grateful. You guys motivate me to keep going, and not give up when times get tough. I promise I am going to make you proud. Thank you, Thank you, and Thank you!!

Table of Contents

Day 1 – What's your story?

Day 2 – Walking in Your Purpose

Day 3 – Doubt & Fear

Day 4 – Negativity

Day 5 - Forgive & Move on

Day 6 – I Hold Myself Accountable

Day 7 – No More Distractions

Day 8 – Stop Complaining

Day 9 – 21 Days of Fitness

Day 10 – Goals, Goals, Goals

Day 11 – Make every Negative a Positive

Day 12 – It's About Me

Day 13 – Focus on Him

Day 14 – Get Out of Your Comfort Zone

Day 15 – You're Closer than You Think

Day 16 – Stressed Out

Day 17 – Bounce Back

30 Days to a Better Me

Day 18 – Worry about Yourself

Day 19 – Spend Time with People You Love

Day 20 – Don't Be Insecure

Day 21 – Break the Habit

Day 22 – New Season of Increase

Day 23 – Give Back

Day 24 – Have Fun

Day 25 – What They Think of You is None of Your Business

Day 26 – Role Model

Day 27 – I Love Me

Day 28 – Today I Commit

Day 29 – Never Give Up

Day 30 – Live Your Life

21 Days of Fitness

Conclusion

Introduction

If you are reading this book, you are ready to start a new journey to become a better you. So first I would like to say congratulations because this is NOT an easy journey, but a very rewarding one. Just like many of you reading this book, I have struggled with what I felt were imperfections with my body, the struggle to forgive myself and others, and to leave the past in the past. Remember when you were a child, and you had dreams of becoming a teacher, doctor, movie star, or even a singer. What about the time when you were in high school, and you had dreams of becoming a basketball player, a lawyer, or an entrepreneur? Whatever your dreams were, back then there was nothing that could get in the way of your dreams coming true. Some of you were fortunate enough to make your dreams come true, and others had to put their dreams on the back burner. In life, it is so easy to lose your way, and truly be happy. We may have the career we want or the family we want, but still never really experience true happiness. For many years people search to find happiness, not knowing that true happiness comes from within. Once we truly love ourselves, accept our flaws and put God first, we then will be truly happy.

When I finally figured out how to truly love myself, and what was really important in life, my life started changing for the better. I do not have it all figured out now, but one thing that I will say, I pray and ask God for strength to accept things I cannot change, and I put forth 100% effort to change the things I can change. You have to make it up in your mind that you want to make a change. You have to be ready to throw all of the fear, negative thoughts and anything that is keeping you from being a better you, out of the window. Stop being that person, wishing to have a better life and become the person you want to be, and live the life you were destined to live.

In this book you will start the healing process for all of your past hurt, learning to love yourself and forgiving yourself and others. This book is a 30 Day, "Mind & Body Makeover." You can be the prettiest woman alive, but if you are not right on the inside, that beauty doesn't even matter. Life is too short to be anything but happy, and each day I strive to become a better me. I want you to close your eyes and say, "I am ready for the new me, the better me, the healthier me, and I will start holding myself accountable today!"

30 Days to a Better Me

This booked is designed to last 30 days, by doing each activity at the end of each day. This book is designed to create healthy habits, start the healing process from the past, and creating the happy life you want. Each day we will talk about a different subject, and each day has an activity for you to complete. Please take your time and think about the questions, before you answer each question in the activity. It is very important that you are honest when answering the questions, to start your healing process, you must first be honest with yourself. After the 30 days are over, you will not be healed completely, but you would have started the healing process. This book is designed to help you become a better you, by digging deep to see where your insecurities started. Your journal is for you to see. You will also need two poster boards, markers, and magazines to create your vision and goal board on day 10. Good luck on your new journey to becoming a better you. Let's make it to the end, and start living the happy and healthy life you were destined to live.

Day 1

What's Your Story

When I think of my life, and the woman that I have become these quotes instantly comes to mind, "Life is what you make it" and "if you are given lemons make lemonade." Although figuratively speaking I chose to stare adversity in the face to get to this place in my life. Life is designed to have ups and downs however what doesn't kill us make us stronger. We must stay persistent and not allow the undesirable misfortunes to break us. So many of us may have had an affliction or some life debacle where we have felt like giving up because there was no more hope. Just like many of you that are reading this book, I have dealt with insecurities with my body inside and out, struggled with forgiving myself and others, and leaving the past in the past. Unfortunately, I have made bad decisions that have altered the course of my life. If given the opportunity, there may be some things that I would change, however, these life alterations is what made me the woman that I am. It's true I have been bent, but I didn't break. Every issue has been a building block for my story to share and be an encouragement for all who have dealt with calamity in their life. I am a stronger and wiser woman today because of my journey. This journey is an eye opener for me because while traveling it, I realized how strong I am.

The beginning of my story starts with me being conceived by teenage parents. My birth came three days before my mother's fifteenth birthday, and my father was seventeen years old. So I had a few obstacles assigned to my life early on. Fortunately, my mother still lived at home with her mother, so I was blessed to have a very supportive grandmother. Though my mother was very young, she was surrounded by strong women who were an asset to both of our lives growing up together. My mother recognized my talent to sing at a very young age and trained me vocally. Comically but true my mother was my Joe Jackson because she didn't play the radio. At eight years old I sang at my first wedding, and by the age of twelve years old, I wrote and recorded my first song. As the years subsequently passed by, I just continued to work hard and perfect my craft. I auditioned for shows like Making the Band, The Voice, and American Idol. I was very talented and could compete on many different levels however the stars never lined up my way. For whatever the reason was I was never chosen to be the top whatever the number. Not knowing at the time these incidents mounting up was chipping away at my self-esteem in a major way. I was plagued with the incomprehensible fear of failure. I didn't understand why I wasn't good enough. I worked very hard, but wasn't getting the results I felt I deserved. Singing was my comfort zone, and I didn't think I could or wanted to do anything else but sing.

In 2009, I was diagnosed with Guillain-Barre Syndrome, which left me paralyzed and in a wheelchair. February, I was celebrating my 25th birthday and at the end of March, I was laying in the hospital bed not able to feed myself, bathe myself, or even write my name. I went through a life changing experience overnight. So my self-esteem went to an all-time low. I went from singing and dancing to not being able to lift my legs. I was petite all of my life and went from a weight of 115 pounds to 160 pounds; I was very uncomfortable in my new skin. For those that know me knows that I have always proceeded to be camera ready and always had a camera with me. Uncannily different after the weight gain, I was a different person. Below are pictures of my weight gain.

No matter what challenge or obstacle that I was faced with I overcame. I passed each test, and it allowed me to have a testimony to share with the world. With each and every experience that I had gone through, I achieved a more personal and stronger relationship with God. I knew that with God anything was possible. I knew that I couldn't put my trust in man because people would let me down every time. I remember when I was sick in the hospital my disease was so rare, that it had no cure. The doctor's said that it was a chance that I wouldn't be able to walk again or to have children, but God saw differently. If I had listened to the doctors, I probably would have given up. My best friend Terrica told me one day at the hospital, "Science only goes so far, and then God steps in." That stuck with me, and I truly believed that if I worked hard, God would meet me halfway. Now in 2016, I am walking and running with a baby boy that will be two years old this year.

> *2 Chronicles 15:7 But as for you, be strong and do not give up, for your work will be rewarded."*

Activity 1

I want you to write your story. It doesn't have to be ten pages long, but write a glimpse of your life like I did above. I know you are probably wondering, why is it important for me to write my story because no one else is going to read it? Well to answer your question, the story is not for me it is a tool for you to use. Throughout the book we are going to talk about forgiveness, moving on from the past and our insecurities. Your story will give you answers to those unknown questions that you have not been able to answer at one point or another. When you write your story, you are going to write the first thing that comes to your mind. Not knowing before, but my feelings of abandonment came from my father not being in my life. My fears of failure and not being good enough came because I was deeply affected by not ever being chosen for auditions when I tried out. My physical insecurities came from the fact that I had gained so much weight, and the new skin I lived with, I hated. To fix any of your problems, you must first acknowledge what the problem is. For the next 30 days, you are going to dig deep down inside and start to forgive yourself and others. Accept who you are this time in your life and move on from the past. You will have to try not to continue to identify yourself with who you were in your past. Every day there should be a new affirmation to rebuilding your self-esteem.

Day 2

Walking in Your Purpose

Just like a lot of you, I LOVE MONEY, and I have worked some of the worst jobs just to get that paycheck. I have never worked a job that I just absolutely loved and wanted to do for the rest of my life. I have had jobs that I liked, and I felt comfortable with the money and position, but nothing gave me that spark. I know many of you who are reading this now are working jobs that you wished you could quit today, or you love your job, but you don't get paid enough. If that is the case, you are not walking in your purpose. When you are walking in your purpose, you can feel it, and it doesn't feel like work. The reward you receive is money and so much more. A lot of times we get overwhelmed with bills and the jobs we have barely even pay the bills, or you work so much you don't have enough time to enjoy your money. The world is so beautiful, and they're so many things that we have not seen nor done. We were not put on this earth to just work and pay bills. God has a tailor-made assignment for us, and once we complete it, and start walking in our destiny, wonderful things start to happen."

5 "Before I formed you in the womb I knew you, before you were born I set you apart; I appointed you as a prophet to the nations." Jeremiah 1:5

When I started reading my bible and started believing, it was a great feeling to know God had a plan just for me. I felt special because that meant, I didn't have to worry or compete with anyone. I could just only focus on him and his word and allow him to guide my footsteps. I knew that if I put God first, and I gave 100 %, there was no way I could lose. I have always known I had a gift of song, and I had an anointed voice, so I knew I was supposed to sing inspirational music. In 2010, I became a motivational speaker, and I loved being able to inspire and motivate people not to give up. I remember speaking to a teenage female mentoring group and when I finished they wanted me to sign my autograph. I was amazed that telling my story and singing touched so many people. After I learned how to walk again, and lost all of my weight, people came to me with so many health & fitness questions. When I first started my fitness journey, I will never forget my mama said, "Girl, you are probably going to be a personal trainer." I laughed because I thought she was crazy, I could barely walk, so how was I going to be a personal trainer. When I finally found my purpose, there was no doubt in my mind that I was doing the right thing. I could use all of my God-given talents, and create a business where I could motivate people in so many ways. When I sing an inspirational song, tell my story, or teach a fitness class, I feel that spark. It is an incredible feeling to do something I love while helping others. I knew this was something I could do for the rest of my life. I truly felt God blessed me to be a blessing to others, and he didn't give me the strength to learn to walk again just to sit at home. He gave me the strength to walk again so I could be an example and show if you step out in faith and believe in God and work hard anything is possible.

'But get up and stand on your feet; for this purpose I have appeared to you, to appoint you a minister and a witness not only to the things which you have seen, but also to the things in which I will appear to you; Acts 26:16

Activity #2
It is your time to find your purpose. It is time for you to start the assignment that God has for you. Have you

started your assignment, and let fear outweigh your hopes and dreams? We were meant to have a beautiful life, and this is our season. Anything worth having does not come easy. Answer the questions below to find your God-given purpose. You only have 30 seconds to answer each question. Write down the first thing that comes to your mind. Be honest, no one is going to read this but you.

1. What is something that makes you smile? (People, hobbies, activities, event)
2. What is something you love doing so much you lose track of time?
3. What are you naturally good at? (Gifts, Talents, etc.)
4. What do people usually ask you to help them with?
5. What is something you loved doing in the past that you still love?
6. What is something that you do that makes you feel good about yourself
7. What is something you would regret if you never tried?
8. What is your God given purpose?

Day 3

Doubts and Fears

Of all my challenges one of my greatest has been overcoming rejection and failure. For so many years rejection and failure had become synonymous with my life. I must say that I consider myself to be a very driven person and very ambitious. However during the process of trying to reach a goal I would allow doubt and fear to keep me from completing the journey. I hate the idea of rejection and failure so much that I would dismantle the goal that I had dreamed about for so long. For most of my life, I have let my doubt and fear outweigh my goals and dreams. I was so scared of failing that I didn't even want to try, or I would quit when it got tough. So then you must know that writing and completing this book is one of my greatest achievements. When I first decided to write this book, I contemplated over the idea day and night. The truth of the matter is I had to reprocess what was the importance of writing a book. Well I knew I had gone through different challenges in my life, and I was like coal going through the fire and I had come out like a diamond. I had to accept my past and forgive myself for all the bad decisions and choices that I had made in my past.

I thought I was in a good place and had moved on and forgiven myself for all the bad choices that I had made. To my surprise, I began to worry about people not seeing the new me or should I say the better me. I was also afraid that people would not be able to see past my past and think that my life was not worth sharing. Did people care about what I had gone through and how I had overcome many of my obstacles? The reality of it was I had changed, and I knew that I was not the same person any longer. There was nothing left to do but accept who I once was and get past this self-destructive attitude. I procrastinated for a while and then I had to give myself a reality check quick fast and in a hurry. I had to realize that people will continue to talk about you whether you are doing good or bad, so you might as well live your life the way you see fit. I remember looking at Steve Harvey on YouTube, and he said, "Face your fears head on, they're not as big as you think. Once you face a big fear, it only becomes smaller, don't let fear stop you." I was no longer going to allow fear to outweigh my dreams this time. I will renounce the words rejection and failure as it applies to my life. I knew that I had a story and experiences that could help someone. Not saying in any form that all of a sudden one day I just decided that I was going to be able to face all of my fears, but it did mean that I would tackle them one dream and one goal at a time. I decided to learn and grow from my fears, and I refused to let it destroy my peace and happiness.

"So do not fear, for I am with you; do not be dismayed, for I am your God. I will strengthen you and help you; I will uphold you with my righteous right hand." Isaiah 41:10

"When I am afraid, I put my trust in you." Psalm 56:3

Overcoming your fear and doubting yourself is easier said than done. I am not expecting anyone to overcome every fear after reading day 3. I know that it takes time, and it will not happen overnight because most of our fears are built up over a period of time. Everyone will not have the same causes and effects that contributed to that particular fear. For example, as a child, you could have almost drowned in the pool so now you have a fear of swimming and water. However as an adult will you allow that fear to keep you from going on a trip to the beach or a cruise with friends and family because you are afraid to be near water due to what happen to you as a child. As for me my fears were feeling rejected and the idea of failure as I explained in the first part of day 3. I do want you to be aware of your fears, so each day you can pray and ask God for strength to overcome your fears. Before you overcome any fears you first have to acknowledge them, work towards them daily, dig deep and see why you are afraid. If you remember on Day 1, I asked you to write your story so that you could think of your past and experiences. Did something happen in the past that made you afraid to follow your dreams? What happens when you are faced with fear? To figure out a resolution and answer to your questions, you must first identify the cause. Remember, failure is just temporary and the harder you work and learn from your mistakes, the more you will succeed the next time.

Activity 3
The purpose of this activity is to help you acknowledge your fears, and take the necessary steps to overcome your fears. Be 100% honest with yourself, because that is the only way you will be able to overcome.

1. List five of your biggest fears. Why is this a fear?
2. What steps can you take today to overcome your fears?
3. List three of your weaknesses. If you acknowledge and accept your weaknesses for what they are it can boost your confidence and self-esteem.

Day 4

Negativity

"Negativity may knock at your door, but that doesn't mean you have to let it in."

~Author unknown

Negativity was my number one distraction, which held me back from accomplishing many of my goals. I allowed self-pity and other's lack of support get in the way of my dreams. Negativity is contagious, and you have to be careful not to let it in your space. I remember I use to tell people my dreams, and they would always have something to say negative about it. I had more people in my circle that was positive, but the negative comments would always out shadow it. The negativity was holding me back, and I was starting to believe it. It seemed like every time someone would get mad at me they would say something about my handicap. "At least, I can walk" or "You can't even keep your balance, I will push you, and you will fall" were the most popular comebacks most had. The comments about my handicap used to hurt my feelings at first; because I had become very insecure after being diagnosed with Guillain-Barre Syndrome. I knew I had to change that negative aspect of my life. I couldn't be drowned in negativity any longer. I had to remove all negative people in my life, and if they stayed, I had to change the way I reacted to certain situations. When I started to listen to author and keynote speaker Tiphani Montgomery, she spoke on positive affirmation, and how important it was. I started writing positive affirmations on sticky notes and started putting it on my computer desk, and on the bathroom mirror. I started telling myself every day that I was beautiful, I was smart, and I was successful. I started praying more, and I was ready for anything that came my way.

Do not repay evil with evil or insult with insult. On the contrary, repay evil with blessing, because to this you were called so that you may inherit a blessing. 1 Peter 3:9

Negative self-talk is the worst negative mindset. When we say something so many times, we start to believe it. We have to speak positivity in our life. One morning I was strolling through Instagram, and I saw a post that said, "What you think is what you become. What you feel you attract. What you imagine you create. – Buddha" I immediately screened shot the post from my phone and added it to my positive affirmation. I wanted to see that quote every day and remember always to stay positive. I know that being positive every single moment of the day and never getting distracted from it is easier said than done. Trust me, I have my moments, but I have learned to choose my battles, and keep it moving. Speak a positive and happy life into existence.

To rid yourself of negativity, you have to first get a relationship with God. Tell him your problems and even your good moments like you tell your best friend. Be grateful for what you have and focus on your blessings instead of your worries. Read your positive affirmations and your bible daily. If someone comes to you with gossip or negativity, stop them before they start. Surround yourself with positive, like-minded people. You may even have to reevaluate your family and friends. If you only have gossip to talk about with a person, you may need to remove yourself. Remember, you cannot tell everyone your dreams because your vision is not meant to be understood by everyone. From this day forward, no longer allow negativity to affect your life in any way.

Activity 4

1. List two negative things in your life that are distracting you.
2. What is something you can do today to rid yourself of that negative distraction?
3. Take action today and get rid of the negativity in your life that is keeping you from being a better you.

Day 5

Forgive and Move on from the Past

Forgiving people and moving on from the past has been very difficult for me to do in my life. I would always hold on to the past hurt and pain. I would only think about how people did me wrong, or the mistakes I had made, that I couldn't move forward with my life. I was so unhappy with my life, and it caused me to feel like I needed validation from others. I didn't understand why people were cruel and cold-hearted, and I was ashamed of my mistakes, so it was even harder for me to forgive myself. As a child, I always had issues dealing with my father's absence. I never understood why he didn't want to be a part of my life, and I only had bad memories. The older I got, the more I realized I couldn't continue to hold on to that hatred in my heart. It wasn't an easy task to forgive him; it seemed like every time I got over one thing something else bad would happen. It was after I started reading my Bible, I realized and understood the importance of forgiving him, myself and others. After reading the following scriptures and a lot of prayers, I slowly started forgiving my father, myself and others. Once I started forgiving myself, I could forgive others.

*Matthew 6:14-15 says, "**14** For if you forgive men when they sin against you, your heavenly Father will also forgive you. **15** But if you do not forgive men their sins, your Father will not forgive your sins."*

*John 1:9 **9** If we confess our sins, he is faithful and just and will forgive us our sins and purify us from all unrighteousness."*

*Acts 3:19 **19** Repent, then, and turn to God, so that your sin may be wiped out, that times of refreshing may come from the Lord."*

      I have a long list of mistakes I have made in the past, and Lord knows I need his forgiveness. How can I expect God to forgive me if I cannot forgive others who have sinned against me? I had never looked at it like that before; I would only think of my feelings. I knew that if God had forgiven me for all of my sins, that it was ok for me to forgive myself. I didn't love myself or value myself like I should have when I was growing up, so I made a lot of mistakes. It was so hard for me to forgive myself because I was seeking validation from everyone else, and some of them hadn't forgiven me for my past. First impressions sometimes last a lifetime, and people who don't have that relationship with God are not going to see the importance of forgiving others. Somebody from my past once told me, "I am proud of you because you have changed and I didn't see this coming." I didn't know how to take that statement because I hadn't truly forgiven myself for my past. I should have taken that as a compliment because I did make a change for the better, but I had taken offense because they brought up the past that I was still ashamed of. Why couldn't they have just said, "I am proud of you," instead of adding the extra? Was it because they still looked at me like the girl I was in the past? Why did I even care what someone else thought about me? When you do not forgive yourself and others, it causes so much damage in so many of areas in your life, and you don't even realize it. Not believing you can change will always hinder you from living your true happy life you are destined to live.

"Remember not the former things, not consider the things old."

Isaiah 43:18

"I press on toward the goal for the prize of the upward call of God in Christ Jesus."

Philippians 3:14

When I was on my first forgiving spree, I felt like a fool afterwards, because it was the same situation as before. They didn't change, so I became bitter again and wished I would have never forgiven them in the first place. My feelings would hurt all over again, and mama told me to accept people as they were and keep it moving. I had to learn another way to forgive. The bible said we had to forgive others, but he didn't say we had to continue being best friends. As the old saying by the author Randall Terry says, "Fool me once shame on you, fool me twice shame on me." It is okay to forgive someone and move on. It is okay to forgive that person, but love yourself enough to know that you deserve so much better.

"The righteous keep moving forward, and those with clean hands become stronger and stronger." Job 17:9

Activity 5
1. List two things that you need to forgive yourself for that is holding you back from reaching your full potential?
2. List two people that you need to forgive in your life? Reach out to them.

Day 6

I hold myself Accountable

Understanding the importance of accountability has the potential to be tricky. To be accountable, you may have to admit that you are wrong, or you may have to accept some truths about yourself that you may not want to recognize. Before you can truly hold yourself accountable, you have to conquer some of your doubt and fears you may have about yourself which we covered on day 3. That is only the start of the path of accountability. You are going to have to accept who you are and know that you are flawed just like everyone else, and that is where forgiveness comes in which we discussed on day 5. Even with understanding that part of the process I had one more thorn to bypass and it was pride. Pride was the booger of all boogers for me to put it mildly. It was my mission not to ever humble myself or to say I am sorry.

I have always been talented, and I was raised to be a dreamer. My family told me that I could do anything I put my mind to, but my nemesis has been my nasty attitude. I have always felt I could say and do what I wanted. When I was younger and even some of my adult years, my attitude was terrible. By the time, I was twenty-one I was in rare form. When I was able to say, "I'm grown," that was it. However before then when I was a teenager, one of my favorite aunts, told my mama that she believed in me, and she would spend her last to help me pursue my singing, but my attitude was too bad. I don't think, I even cared back then but hearing that same story as an adult made me feel remorseful and ashamed. The truth of the matter is I know that she would have been that blessing for me that I needed to get to the next level. In time, I started looking at my life, and I wasn't happy with the way it was going. I knew that I had to make some changes, and I had to first look in the mirror. It was no secret that I had a bad attitude, I would have friends that would tell me, that I should think before I spoke, or I didn't have to say everything that I was thinking. Sometimes I would care and other times I wouldn't care what they said or thought. It has been since I have been an adult that I knew I had to change my attitude. I was starting not to like the person I had become. If you made me mad and said something I didn't like, I would hit you below the belt, and not think twice about it. Well, it all changed, when I started hurting people that I loved. One day I got into an argument with one of my brothers, and he made me so furious, that the words began to flow, and I was taking jabs. Well, of course, brothers and sisters have disagreements and make up, so a few years later we got into another argument, and he brought up the old comments that I had said years ago. At that moment, I realized how far words could penetrate and I wished I could have taken those hurtful words back that I had said earlier, but I couldn't. It hit me then that I had to watch the things that I said to people when I was mad. At that moment, I knew I had to hold myself accountable for my attitude. Realizing also that attitude is altitude, and I wanted to soar.

> *"I did then what I knew how to do. Now that I know better, I do better."* ~Maya Angelou

Looking back over my life I am confident in knowing that I lost many opportunities because of my attitude and tarnished some relationships. I have always been a hard worker, but never reaching the success I felt like I should have reached. It was once I started holding myself accountable that doors started opening. I knew that I had to work hard, and not depend on someone else to work harder for me for my success. I am also aware that some people won't allow you to change and will only want to remember your bad. But as we discuss on day 25 it's none of your business what they think of you. Most importantly I knew that if I wanted to be blessed I had to try to become more like Christ and Christ was not walking around with a nasty attitude. Your attitude will take you a long way.

Activity 6
1. Is your life going the way that you want it to go? Is there something that you need to start holding yourself accountable for today?
2. In your journal, write one thing in your life that you need to hold yourself accountable and start working on it today.

Day 7

No More Distractions

A distraction is something that takes your attention away from something that you supposed to be doing. It can make a person unfocused, or it can be a diversion from a problem maybe something to amuse or entertain you. There are only twenty-four hours in a day with one million things to do. I have normal activities just like everyone else such as being a mother, a business woman, a housekeeper, a cook and all the other things that go along with being a busy woman in today's society. Often I get so busy, and my mind starts to ponder on the things that I didn't do. It may be a fitness video I should have posted or maybe a simple run to the store to buy milk. Ironically I would reset and think about my day to figure out where the time went. After considerable thought, it came down to social media. Apparently my biggest distraction is social media, mostly Facebook. If you know me personally, and we are friends on Facebook, you know that I am addicted. I would spend hours at a time on social media divulging in posting or being nosey reading someone else's business. I know that I am not the only one because I see my newsfeed. Social media is just my distraction, but yours could be an array of things. I have countless acquaintances that I dialogue with often, and their distractions are somewhat different from mind. Whatever your distraction is, it is time to get rid of it.

Social Media had taken on another life for me instantaneously. I was always on my phone checking Facebook. I would be working on the computer, and I couldn't complete many of my responsibilities because of notifications from Facebook. If I received a notification ironically, it would take priority. I knew that it was appropriate that I took some time from Facebook and focused. I gradually eased away from Facebook, and it wasn't easy, but I stayed persistent. I deleted apps that would instigate temptation. However, I disciplined myself only to be on Facebook when all of my work was complete, or I needed to reach out to someone for the purpose of business. When I decided to limit my time off of social media, it added more minutes to my day that incidentally was lost in the course of the day. I started working on completing the things that were on my goal board. I stopped gossiping about what I saw on Facebook with my friends, eventually I started getting things done. Instead of spending hours strolling through Facebook worrying about someone else's business I just simply started minding my own business. I was determined to prepare for the upcoming year. Like the saying says, "If you stay ready, you don't have to get ready." Now, don't get me wrong, I still get distracted at times, but I handle it in a different way. I had to set boundaries with myself and other people. If it wasn't positive, I knew that I could not allow it to take any of my time.

Activity 7

I want you to challenge yourself and try to figure out where you are losing time in your day with undesirable distractions. First write down a to-do list for the day. At the end of the day see what was not completed and then figure out everything that you did for the entire day whether it is gossiping, reality shows or maybe even an unscheduled nap. Calculate how much time you spend on each and you will see where the time went. In the next 24 hours replace the lost time with spending more time working on the things that you need to do for the day. I will also encourage you to carve out some time on positive reading such as the Word of God or a devotional. Trust me; you will see a difference in your life.

Day 8

Stop Complaining

First of all, let me say, I cannot endure being around a person who complains all of the time. I know that sounds insensitive, and I know everyone has a moment where they need to vent; consequently, those aren't the people I am talking too. I am talking about the people who complain about everything, I am sure you know of a few people like that, you may even be that person.

Philippians 2:14 says, Do all things without grumbling or questioning.

Ephesians 4:29 says, Let no corrupting talk come out of your mouths, but only such as is good for building up, as fits the occasion, that it may give grace to those who hear.

When I first became paralyzed, I was thinking why me and what am I going to do? I remember around the same time, one of my peers had a really bad motorcycle accident and had one of his legs amputated. His situation gave me a different perspective on how I was feeling. Here I was sad and complaining, and here was someone who had their leg removed and gratefully I still had both of my legs. At that point, my diagnosis was that I may never walk again. Instantly I had to make a choice to complain about my situation or fight the odds. As time progressed, I began to get the feeling back in my legs and hands, and it was very painful. I would tell my mom how much pain I was in, and she would say, "Thank God for the pain had you not had the pain you would still be paralyzed with no feeling." Another example of not complaining is one about my grandmother whom I loved dearly. She was a hard working woman who lost her leg to diabetes. Instead of complaining and waiting on the Social Security to kick in she wore her prosthetic leg and went back to work proudly. For that reason alone I have zero tolerance for people who complain, I mean it, I do not want to hear it, believe me, I am not trying to be insensitive. I have an autoimmune disorder and many mornings, I do not feel good or want to get out of the bed, but I do. I look at my mother who has Lupus another autoimmune disorder, and her weakness is 50 times worse than mine, so how can I complain. She works two jobs an active wife, mother, and grandmother, and you hardly ever hear her complain. You have to surround yourself with like-minded positive people. Complaining is a negative spirit and is not of the Lord and it is very contagious. If you are amongst a group of people who only complain, you will be the next person in the conversation complaining. Surround yourself with people who are go-getters and hardworking people. Make every negative situation into a positive situation, which we will talk about on Day 11.

Complaining doesn't help with change, nor fix your problems. Below I am going to list a lot of Bible verses that you can write down and read daily. The only one who can truly help you with your problems and all of the things you are complaining about is God. I have to read my Bible continuously and stay in an environment that is free of complaining. Stay focused on God's word so you won't have room for anything else.

1 Thessalonians 5:18 says, Give thanks in all circumstances; for this is the will of God in Christ Jesus for you.

Numbers 11:1-4 says, And the people complained in

the hearing of the Lord about their misfortunes, and when the Lord heard it, his anger was kindled, and the fire of the Lord burned among them and consumed some outlying parts of the camp. Then the people cried out to Moses, and Moses prayed to the Lord, and the fire died down. So the name of that place was called Taberah, because the fire of the Lord burned among them. Now the rabble that was among them had a strong craving. And the people of Israel also wept again and said, "Oh that we had meat to eat."

Philippians 2: 14-16 says Do all things without grumbling or questioning, that you may be blameless and innocent, children of God without blemish in the midst of a crooked and twisted generation, among whom you shine as lights in the world, holding fast to the word of life, so that in the day of Christ I may be proud that I did not run in vain or labor in vain.

Proverbs 17:22 A joyful heart is good medicine, but a crushed spirit dries up the bones.

Activity 8

1. List three things you complain about all of the time, that you can fix.

2. Instead of complaining figure out a way to fix the problem.

Day 9

21 Days of Fitness

I know many of you are excited about fitness, but most of you probably want to put the book down now. Well, we have for the most part got our mind right, and talked about our fears, doubts, negativity, forgiveness and more. While we are working on mending our insides, now let's work on the outside as well. I know many of us deal with insecurities with our appearance. So this book is a one-stop shop for a better you. I have created a 21 Day plan for you guys, and it will work if you do it. I have made a 21 Day Workout plan and meal plan guide for you to follow. I have even taken pictures of each workout, so you can't use the excuse that you don't know what to do. I have provided healthier choices, and I have also shared some of my favorite healthy meals; many of my clients have tried them and loved them. Not only do we need to look good to feel good about ourselves, but it is very important to live a healthy lifestyle.

I know when most people hear healthy living, they

get discouraged just thinking about it. I am not approaching this as if healthy living or making a lifestyle change will be easy, but the rewards are so worth it and rewarding. When we think of losing weight or being on a diet, we fail because we think of all of the limitation of the foods we can't eat. I had to stop doing that, and gradually limit the unhealthy foods and substitute with healthy foods I did like. Instead of trying to do a quick fix and lose weight fast, make it a lifestyle.

Unfortunately, most of the time when you lose weight fast; you gain it right back because you never learned discipline in the first place. How can you keep off the weight, if you didn't learn to utilize good habits with working out and eating healthy? During this time, Pinterest and Google should be your best friends. The food that I have provided, you may not like or already have healthy food choices that work for you. However, I will give you a guideline for all of the good and bad foods. In the back of the book, they're instructions on how to follow my 21 Days of fitness workout and meal plan. Eating healthy is 70 percent to Working out 30 percent.

I know working out is a challenge for most of you because you lack the motivation needed to do it daily.

You hate the soreness that comes after the workout, and the pain of the workout. Like they say, "No pain, No gain." Living a healthy and fit lifestyle is mental. You can hire a personal trainer, a health coach and any other kind of fitness guru, but if your mind isn't present then it doesn't matter. When I very first started my business back in 2013, I would get discouraged quickly, because I didn't know why I would keep some people and others would continuously drop off. I would cheat myself and lower my prices thinking that would keep people engaged. The reality of it is spending $10 is just like spending $100, to someone who is truly not interested in making the change. So you have to make sure you are committed to living a healthy lifestyle.

Healthy living can be fun if you make it. There are so many fitness classes from Zumba, Water Aerobics, and Group training classes, to One on One classes, you also have Pole dancing classes and Twerk classes. So there is something out there for all types of people. I have provided you with basic workouts you can do in the comfort of your home or at a park by yourself or with a friend or two. Don't allow another year to go by and you still have the same insecurities that you had the previous years all because you are lazy and unmotivated. Start 2016 off to a great start, and become a better you on the inside and out.

Activity 9
Below are some questions that you need to answer to get you on track to becoming fit and just a healthier you.

1. What time is the best time for you to work out? Many times our biggest excuse is that we are too busy, and we do not have time to work out, but you make time for what you want. In the mornings are the best times for me, because I am getting it out of the way, and I don't have to worry about it for the rest of the day.
2. What are your favorite workouts? Do you enjoy long walks at the Park or a short jog? Do you enjoy dancing or group workouts, or would you rather work one on one? Find whatever works for you.
3. What are your favorite fruits and vegetables? What are your favorite foods? After you have listed all of your foods, check my list in the back of the book and if it is not listed, google a substitution that will come close to fulfilling your taste buds.

Day 10

Goals, Goals & Goals

If you follow me on social media, you already know that making goal boards and vision boards are paramount in my life. Right now I have a goal board that is vast in size above my desk that I have to look at every day. No matter how old you are, it is never too late or too early to start working on your goals. I know some of my family and friend's give me a bizarre look and do not comprehend the sacrifice I make for my business, but it is not for them to understand. When I make a really big goal, I move in silence, and only tell a few people, because you cannot tell everyone your dreams. It is Day 10, so by now you know that quotes and biblical scriptures are an enormous part of my life. Below are a few of my favorite quotes that can get your day underway.

"Never give up on a dream just because of the time it will take to accomplish it. The time will pass anyway." – Earl Nightingale

"Many things aren't equal but everyone gets the same 24 hours a Day, 7 Days a Week. We make time for what we truly want." –Unknown

"We are not given a good life. We are given life. And it's up to you to make it good or bad." – Unknown

"The best time to start was yesterday. The next best time is NOW." –unknown

I was introduced to goal and vision boards back in 2012 when I had a guest speaker come to one of my mentoring group meetings. The speaker had the girls, cut out pictures of things that they wanted to accomplish or acquire in their life. I fell in love with the idea and wanted to create one for myself. I crafted a vision board, and positioned things on it like a house, a car, family, a building for my future business, but that wasn't enough. I needed to figure out how I was going to acquire the house, car and everything else that I desired. Once I completed the goal board, I had to write out how I was going to accomplish this task. Through trial and error, I had to figure out the kind of board that would work best for me.

At the beginning of 2013, no longer pondering I decided that I would attend school to become a personal trainer. I knew that I had to get focused, and get my body in shape the way I wanted it to be. I continued to work out more and tried different healthy meals. During this time, I only had healthy foods in my fridge and pantry, either you ate clean with me, or you had to buy your food. I made a fitness board, with all of the goals I wanted to reach, and I kept track of my progress.

By now my body resembled what I had envisioned it to be. February 2013 I was attending school for personal training. Everything was going as planned, and initiating the goal board was causing me to thrive.

Subsequently, I had my son in 2014; I had to adapt to motherhood and figure out what was best for my son and me. I was working and would make goal boards throughout the year, but eventually, I made the goal board that would pose the greatest difference in May 2015. Although half of the year was over, I was going to be prepared for 2016. I was going to have the product and was just going to push it and grind it out in 2016. Before I made this goal board, I ascertained more thought in how I would design it. I didn't just want to gape in a magazine and begin cutting; I needed it planned out deliberate. I knew for me to go to the next level with my business, I had to get my body in shape, and I had to find alternative ways to make money. I knew that I couldn't be in the same place the following year.

I separated the board in three sections that were most important to me. The first section, I took a before picture of me and all of my personal fitness goals. Even though most people saw me as being fit, I hated the way my body looked. I wanted to look like I did before the baby, and I was determined. The middle section included everything that I wanted to accomplish in my business, starting with writing a book, a recipe book, forming boot camps, and videos. The last section included personal goals that I wanted to have for my family. I wanted to get 50% of the board completed if not all of it. My goal was to prepare for 2016, so I inadvertently put it in a place that I would have to look every day. There was not a day that went by, where I didn't sit at my desk for a couple of hours at a time. So if you are reading this book, that means I accomplished more than 80% of my goals and the other 20% is cooking in the oven, and will be ready soon. Remember, never allow anyone to discouraged you or become doubtful of yourself and your goals. If you believe and put the work in it, it will happen for you, I am a witness. Most of the time when I have goals, I do not know how I am going to do it, or how I am going to fund it, but I truly believe if I put 150 percent in, God will meet me more than halfway.

Activity 10

First I want you to make a vision board. Think about where you want your life to be in a year, and in 5 years. Look through a few magazines, and cut every picture that relates to your vision. It may be children, a wedding, a house, car, etc. Make it colorful, and place it somewhere you will see it daily.

Now that your vision board is complete you will now have to make your vision a reality? I want you to start off small when you are approaching your goals. It is good to dream big, believe me, I do it all of the time, but you have to be realistic. I would make so many goals that I would not reach and become discouraged. So, I want you to start a 30-day goal board, and when you complete that, make more goals.

1. List three goals that you want to work on within the next 30 days
2. Make a poster board, and write all of your goals on the board including steps and deadlines of when you will finish. By the time you finish this book, your 30 days won't be up yet, but as soon as your 30 Days are almost over and you have completed your realistic goals, make another one. After your 30 Day Goal board, make a bigger goal and complete it in 3 months, after you finish that, make a bigger goal and complete in 6 months and one year.

"If you plan to fail, you fail to plan." ~ Benjamin Franklin

Day 11

Make Every Negative a Positive

I know that it is easier said than done, to make a negative situation into a positive. I think it is human nature to get dismayed when things do not go our way. However, it is left up to us if we allow it to make or break us. I had met numerous people over the years that said they don't know if they could have been as strong as I was when I paralyzed. You never know the depth of your strength you possess until you face an incredible challenge. Even in the worst situation, you can turn it into a positive. For example, let's use a bad relationship that is something I am sure we can relate to at some point or another. Enduring the bad breakup left you distraught, and you probably felt like a great deal of the time was unproductive, but instead consider it as a learning experience. Life is full of test that evidently you will either pass or fail. Use all of your failures as learning opportunities.

"Every test in our life makes us bitter or better, every problem comes to make us or break us. The choice is

ours whether we become victims or victorious."
~Unknown

In school, we learn first before we take the test. In life, we take the test first before we learn." ~Unknown

In 2009 when I became paralyzed, I never wanted to question God, but I did wonder why he chose me. Guillain-Barre Syndrome was a disease so rare that it didn't have a cure. Then it was like 1-2 people out of every 100,000 people that were diagnosed with it. As I was going through that situation, I was so perplexed and confused. I was a 25-year old who loved singing and dancing. But now, I was incapable of walking and moving my legs, I could not feed myself or even write my name. At this time, I realized I had taken so much for granted. You expect to just wake up the next morning, and everything is the same as it was the day before. Never in a million years did I think my feet would start hurting, and a month later, I would be wheelchair bound. I was going through a horrendous time, and my stepfather told me to read Jeremiah 29:11, and after I had read that one verse, I wanted to read more. I read so much that I started to believe that something good was going to come out of the situation. I started focusing on all of the things that I could do and stopped focusing on the things that I was not able to do.

In 2013, I was doing so much better though I wasn't a 100%. I had a great deal of people following my story and asking how I lost the weight I had gained. Admirably asking what did I do to learn how to walk again? I had always loved helping people, and I felt God had chosen me to go through this particular test because he knew I was strong enough to get through and I could use my testimony to inspire the world. I desired to be an example and show people that if they didn't give up and worked hard anything was possible. I remember the first time I spoke to a mentoring group, I knew motivational speaking was something I could do forever. After realizing what God's purpose was for me, I knew then I would use every negative situation and purposely turn it into a positive situation that would not only help me but help others as well.

Think of a negative situation that has truly been life changing. It may be something that you are holding in which is causing you to be held back; there are no limits on what it could be. Instead of holding all of that hurt and pain inside, help others by letting them know they are not alone. For example, if you were raped or abused when you were younger, instead of being ashamed and full of hate, use it in a positive way and help other females young and old get through their situation. Remember no one has the power of judgment only our Lord and Savior has that power. One of my favorite singers is the late Aaliyah, and she has a song called "Try Again" and she sang, "If first you don't succeed, dust yourself off and try again." Unquestionably this is how you have to look at all mistakes and failures. You always have to think positive; a positive attitude equals a positive outcome.

Activity 11

1. Think of two negative situations that are currently going on in you life.
2. What could you do to turn your negative situations into positive ones? Start applying it today.

Day 12

It's About Me

One of my greatest attributes is that I am a natural caregiver. I have always loved making people happy in some form of fashion. It gives me great joy to put a smile on someone's face. I enjoy giving back to the community whether it is helping the homeless or helping my Pastor with his political campaign. However, the flip side of that is that sometimes taking care of myself is put on the back burner. It becomes easy not to think of myself and only think of others and what you can do to make them happy. Another point to consider is that how you look is a representation of how you feel. What I mean is if you look like crap you will feel like crap. Take the time to comb your hair and fix yourself up even if you are not going anywhere. I have a cousin whose finances are very limited, but she keeps her nails done at all times by giving herself weekly manicures and pedicures.

When is the last time, you did something for yourself? When is the last time you spent the whole day just pampering or only worrying about you? I know so many times we get caught up in life worrying about our kids, mate, and family that we do not make time to make us happy. I know that most schedules are busy, you are working many hours and trying to manage a household and more, but no matter what you have to make time for yourself. Sometimes I do get overly focused on work that I don't take the time to have any fun. When I started my business, I was all in just constantly grinding it out. I then became a mother, and that added to the fusion of not focusing on me. After I had my son and I went full time with my business it became worst. I was so focused on making money and adjusting to motherhood, that I was not living. I had to realize everyone deserves a day just to relax.

"Everybody dies, but not everybody lives" ~ Drake

We were born to be happy, enjoy ourselves and live every day like it is our last. It took me a moment to realize this incredulous point. I stayed in the house so much that I started to feel uncomfortable when I would go out especially after my son was born. I don't know why I thought it would make me look like an unfit mother if I went out and had fun. My mother would say, "Meisha, if I were your age and looked like you, I wouldn't be sitting in the house, you are too young for that." So my friends and I started a "Ladies

Night Out", one to two Thursdays out of the month. I know one to two days a month doesn't sound like a lot, but it was enough for me. I had something to look forward too, and I started to feel a balance. So if you are as I was before, you have to start living and making certain days just for you. Don't allow your finances to stop you from having your day. You do not have to spend money to make the day about you. Making the day about you just doesn't have to be a ladies night out. I know many of you do not like going to clubs (neither do I) and you do not like to go to lounges or bars (I love them), but you can find something you want to do. My mother likes to go to Karaoke to sing, but a day of fun for her would to be left alone, lounging reading her books or listening to her audiobooks. Some weekends, I would get a babysitter just to sit at home and not do anything but what I wanted to do. So if they're days where you wake up, and you just need time to yourself, it is okay, you are not the only one. Every day I try to set aside at least 30 minutes to an hour to do absolutely nothing but put my legs up and relax. Some days I use my son's nap time as my break, and other times I spend it with my son eating popcorn or grapes. Just remember to make time doing something you want to do.

"Enjoy the little things in life, because one day you will

look back and realize they were big things." ~The Vow

Activity 12

I want you to plan something two to four days in the next 30 days just for you. You can get a manicure and a pedicure, a massage, have a ladies night or planned to have a day where you are home alone doing absolutely nothing. Also, put aside, at least, thirty minutes to an hour a day to just relax.

Day 13

Focus on Him

Have you every just got by yourself and just talked to God, like you talk to your best friend. I know that might sound peculiar to some people, but having a relationship with God is the best relationship to have. I sometimes reminisce about times when I was younger, and I would be at church and I would feel the spirit and wouldn't express myself because I was afraid people would look at me curiously. At that time, I didn't know God like I know him now. I would only pray when I needed something from him, I didn't give him the glory that he deserved. Everyone has a different type of relationship with God, and you do not have to attend church to have one. I was raised in the church, so the foundation was there at that point I just wasn't acknowledging it.

I grew up going to church and singing Gospel music. At that time, I was just singing words not knowing what the meaning was behind the lyrics. When I got into my teens, I didn't go to church, and I probably prayed when the mood hit. Back then I didn't love or value myself as I should have, so understanding that God's love for me was so great seemed absurd. Now I knew about God, but I truly didn't know him. I found a relationship with God when I was 25 years old. That is when I knew for myself that God was in the miracle business, and with him all things were possible. I had grown up singing about how good God was, but I didn't understand for myself then. It took me to get to my lowest, where no one else was able to help me, and I had to turn to God. I could remember my mom saying, "God has a way of sitting you down." The God I found showed up and showed out!!!!!!

I remember lying in the hospital bed crying because two rehabs had denied me from being able to go to their center. I couldn't walk, feed myself or bathe myself, and I couldn't understand why they denied me the opportunity I needed because I was in bad shape. I remember I was alone in my hospital room, and I started praying to God. I asked him to please help me to understand why I was going through what I was going through, and how to handle it. For the next few days, I continued my treatment and therapy. I was getting better every day, and I continued to pray. I would never forget, I had one more treatment and two more physical therapy sessions. Before I started my treatment, my physical therapist came in the room with a walker and told me that I was going to get up and walk with my walker. I was scared, and I did not think I could do it, just days before I could not even hold myself up with the walker. To my surprise, I pulled myself up with the walker and started walking the longest distance that I ever had. I was so happy and in disbelief of what had just taken place. The next time I spoke to the doctor, he said, "After your last treatment and therapy sessions, you can go home. Your therapist said that you had made a tremendous improvement, and she didn't think you needed to go to rehab." I couldn't believe what I was hearing; here I was crying and sad because I didn't understand why the rehabs denied me, not knowing that God had better plans for me. I knew then that if I believed, worked hard; God would meet me more than halfway.

Now, my relationship with God is better than

ever. Sometimes I fall short, and I need a reality check on what I know God can do. I pray every day, through the good times and the bad. Every morning I wake up, and I say thank you. I downloaded the Bible app on my phone, and I get Bible verses sent to my phone every morning. I also pick different bible plans to help me get through and to keep me strong. I make it a priority to thank God, pray and read his word and talk to him every day. I am no longer ashamed to praise God because I know without him nothing is possible.

"God has no phone, but I talk to him. He has no Facebook, but he is still my friend. He does not have Twitter, but I still follow him" ~Unknown

"God loves you more in a moment than anyone could in a lifetime" ~Unknown

Activity 13
Set aside some time today and every day to spend with God. Build your relationship with him, and trust him. Man will always let you down at some point, but God will never leave your side. You cannot think of a time, where you needed God, and he didn't come through. (Besides Death)

Day 14

Get out of your comfort zone

Are you an introvert and a loner? I think the way people are set up these days; everyone would rather stay to themselves which may not always be healthy. I use to loathe change because I hated to be taken out of my comfort zone. If it made me feel nervous or uncomfortable, I wouldn't do it, and I would make up every excuse why I felt like I shouldn't do it. In my opinion, that is why many people stagnate in their life because they are afraid of change. Why change if you have been living this way your whole life? Like the saying, "If it is not broke don't fix it." People are afraid that if they change, they may fail. I know that is one of the things that held me back. I was afraid to do different things and step out of my comfort zone because I felt like I would look stupid or I may fail. However, after being sick and tired of not being able to live life and have the success I felt I should have had, I started to make some changes.

One of the first times I stepped out of my comfort zone was when I moved to Charlotte, North Carolina with my job. I was so scared to move away from my family and start over in a new city and state. I told myself, just go up there and if you do not like it, at least, you can say you tried something different. I wanted to start fresh with my business and meet new people to build my clientele. Charlotte hosted a big fitness expo, and I wanted to go really bad. My child's father didn't want to go with me, so that meant if I went I had to go alone. In the past, you couldn't have paid me to go anyplace alone, but I did it, and I felt good about it. After I had gone, I only found out that it was much easier than I thought, and now I will go places alone all of the time.

At times when I would drive, I would see people standing in the street holding up signs trying to get everyone's attention by waving or dancing around. When I would ride by them, I would also laugh and say I would never do that. Well, one day I was volunteering for my Pastor as he was running for city council, and the manager asked me and another lady to go and stand in front of the apartment building by the street, hold the flag, smile, and wave. At first, I laughed and looked at her crazy because I knew she could not have been serious because in my mind I wasn't going to be waving on the side of the street. However, it was something about this ladies approach that I couldn't say no to her, so I did it. I went to the front of the apartments, standing by the big sign, waving and smiling when cars rode by. At first it was very uncomfortable because men would slow their cars down; some people would make eye contact with me and still not speak. As I kept on doing it, it became easier for me to wave and smile, and slowly I started to get out of my comfort zone. Don't get me wrong, I am not saying that I am going to look for a job as a sign holder, but I did something different and conquered a fear. I don't consider myself to be anti-social, but sometimes it is hard for me to speak to people without getting nervous. Now I'm not talking about speaking to a person in passing. Ok, for instance, how can I be in a business of networking but uncomfortable with talking to people about my business? I was a little timid when the initial conversation would start and eventually would ease into a more comfortable place. However, with becoming more comfortable with who I am and whose I am I have transitioned well.

"Move out of your comfort zone. You can only grow if you are willing to feel awkward and uncomfortable when you try something NEW." ~Brian Tracey

"If you want something you've never had, then you've got to do something you've never done." ~Unknown

Activity 14

I want you to step out of your comfort zone, and do something you have never done before. If it scares you, then you should try it. Think of something that can help you progress in your personal or business life, and take a chance. Stepping out of your comfort zone could be things like: Speaking in public, starting the career of your choice, going in public by yourself, etc. Just remember if you want to grow in life, you must accept change.

Day 15

You are closer than you think

Have you ever just felt like all of your hard work was in vain? If so, you are not alone. People work hard for years, and still feel like they haven't received their payoff. Are you walking in your purpose and doing what God is leading you to do? There have been so many times in life, where I felt like I was working hard for nothing. I felt like I was running, but I was not going anywhere. I would get so far and give up for whatever the reason because I did not see rapid results. During this process, I have learned and truly feel that if you walk in your purpose, you are on the road to success. It is when we become distracted that our plans go wrong. Always remember to keep the faith, pray and allow God to lead you so that you will have a clear vision and understanding of your path.

When I was in my early twenties, I always felt like I was going to be the next big R&B sensation. I felt like I was one of the best, I wrote my songs, and I went out and did shows. I would open up and perform for a big artist that came in town, and I felt like my time was coming. Vocally, I was better than many singers locally and famous. So I couldn't understand why I would come close, but I couldn't reach the level, I felt like I deserved. I wanted to give up so many times, and just stop singing, and for a minute, I did not want to sing at all because I was tired of what I looked at as a failure. Now that I look back, I wasn't ready for that type of success mentally, and I wasn't going in the right direction. So it was probably best, but most importantly it wasn't in God's plan.

After I had learned to walk again, I had a close relationship with God, and I felt like he placed me in the right direction to walk in my purpose. Before my sickness, I thought that I could only become successful as an R&B artist. I hardly went to church at the time, neither singing gospel or inspirational music was definitely out of the question. Woody Allen said, "If you want to make God laugh, tell him about your plans." So, I am sure God had a good laugh about me and my plans. When I stepped out on faith and went full time with my business, it was scary, but I had more time to focus on building my business, and it felt good. I remember in November of 2015, I was talking to one my friends about how good God was to me. I had been laid off of my job in May of 2015, and with only a couple of faithful clients, I had been okay financially. God would always bless me with constant monetary gifts, or some help. I was always scared not to work a real 9 to 5 because I thought the financial struggle would be too much to handle, but I was wrong. I finally stepped out on faith, and I was allowing God to help guide me with every decision I made. I saw the light at the end of the tunnel, and I truly believed that my hard work would pay off if I kept going.

When you are tired and feel like giving up, you have to reevaluate your situation. Ask yourself, "Are you walking in your purpose and allowing God to lead you?" If you are walking by faith and not by sight, you will know the feeling when you are walking in your purpose. I am not saying that you won't go through struggles, but you will use them as learning opportunities. You will still love what you do even if you had to do it for free. So do not give up, when times get tough. Nothing worth having will come easy, and when you get the success, you have to work harder to keep it. When you are going through a tough time, remember that God won't put more on you than you can handle. I had had moments when I thought that it may be smarter just to get a real 9 to 5 because I knew that I would get a guaranteed check. Then, I thought about being laid off from my last two jobs and having to figure out, out of nowhere how I was going to have to pay my bills. I would rather work hard for myself versus working hard for somebody that could fire or lay me off at any given moment. When I felt like giving up, I just remembered why I started my journey, and that I had to keep going and each day I would be closer than I was yesterday.

Activity 15
Whenever you feel like giving up, ask yourself the following questions.

1. Are you walking in your purpose?
2. Are you doing everything in your ability to make your dreams come true?

Day 16

Stressed Out

I am sure that everyone has heard the saying, "Too blessed to be stressed" but we all need a reality check sometime. It is so easy to let negativity and nonsense stress you out and out shadow all of your blessings. It may not even be apparent that you are stressed. It could be normal for your life to be hectic and all over the place. We all have things going on; it could be from unpaid bills, bad relationships, children, jobs, family, health issues and more. However functioning at a high pace can be rewarding for some but it can eventually turn into a stressor. There was a point in my life, where I let any and everything stress me out, I was definitely in a bad place in my life. I wasn't focusing on God and his word, and it was hard for me to find the good in anything. I had to take a break from the world (Social Media) and focus on God. I couldn't allow any more negativity to stress me out. I knew that I needed a reality check fast because I was too blessed to be stressed out about anything. It's a part of my DNA to challenge myself and to conquer different task on time. I have always juggled or multi-task several things at a time, but I never had a balanced life.

One day I woke up extremely overwhelmed. I realized that my hectic life had finally caught up with me. I had become unhappy and stressed out. I had been through so much, and I knew that my current situation could be worse which made it hard to complain so I kept on pushing. There are people who did not even wake up, and there was the time that I woke up and could not even walk, so what was that serious to be stressing over. I wanted to start living a happy life and make great memories. My Mama would always say, "Everything is not an issue. Stop stressing and worrying about things that do not affect your day to day life, and things that are not going to matter even next week." I started praying more, and the more I prayed, the stronger I became. I know you have heard, "If you pray don't worry, and if you worry don't pray." I had heard that saying so many times, and I knew it was true. I wanted to live by that, and truly be grateful and happy. I did not want to be stressed out anymore, and I was the only one that was in control of my happiness.

It is not good to be stressed out because not only

does it affect your day to day life, stress is not good for your health. When you hear people say stress kills, it's true. When I started to make a conscious decision to be happy, I had to become aware of the things that stressed me out. I knew if I talked to certain people, or put myself in certain situations, it would trigger my stress level, so I avoided those situations. I stopped giving time to people who were not deserving of it. I also changed my reaction to situations and realized everything did not deserve a reaction. Growing up, I had a really bad attitude, and I would just fly off the handle when I was upset, and that was not the right approach. I would make situations worse than it had to be. So, once I learned to react differently, and not give attention to ignorant things, my stress level went down. Always remember everything doesn't deserve a reaction.

Every day you are going to be faced with a challenge and it is up to you, how you react. When you wake up in the morning, you are in control of how your day is going to go. If you still were worrying about yesterday, then it is going to affect your day. Wake up in the morning and say thank you God, and pray for a great day and ask that he leads and guide your day. Be thankful and grateful for your current circumstance, because it could always be worse. Instead of stressing over your problems, find a solution so you can figure out a way to eliminate that stress. Some of your stresses can come from the lack of order in your life. So to help me I use goal boards and to do list to get things accomplished in my day. I had to realize I can only do one task at a time even though I can multi-task. Just know its ok to take a break to refresh.

Activity 16

1. Write down two things that you are stressed out about in your life.
2. What are two steps you can take today to eliminate those stresses? Start applying them today?

Day 17

Bounce Back

Everyone has bad days, but you cannot be down forever. I do believe that it is okay to be sad, cry and talk about your problems because holding it in can be dangerous. Do you know someone who always hold everything in, until they explode with anger? Yeah, I know a few people like that, and I have also been that person before. I have a rule about being sad and stressed out too long. Depending on how bad the situation is, you have a max of three days to get it back together and bounce back. I am not saying you have to get over the situation in 3 days, but you have to get up and start moving around again. It serves you no purpose to walk around in self-pity, because the sad thing is, people do not care about your issues. Many mornings I wake up feeling weak or sick because of my auto-immune disorder, and no one cares. No one makes shortcuts for me or goes the extra mile because I have an auto-immune disorder. Life goes on and so does people, so you might as well bounce back and get back on track.

When you live in self-pity or stay stressed out, you are only wasting your time. Time is the worst thing you can waste because you will never get that back. I think the year 2014 was the best but the worst year of my life, it was like a blessing and a curse. In February of 2014, my miracle baby was born, and I was the happiest mom ever, but in July 2014, my then nine-year relationship was over. I was 30 years old, knowing nothing about infants, going through postpartum depression, dealing with my first heartache and still living with an autoimmune disorder. I was hurt and out of my mind that I didn't care about anything. I remember my child's father and I had gotten into a big argument, and I couldn't take it, and I blasted him and everything he did on Facebook. I knew it was the wrong thing to do, but I wanted him to hurt. It took forever for me to forgive myself for that, and I am not sure if I ever did 100 percent, because it did not matter at the end of the day, and no one cared. When you walk in self-pity, and you wear your emotions on your shoulders, it just simply gives people something to gossip and talk about with their family and friends. So do not sit in self-pity too long, I have been there. I spent months crying, wasting time talking about and trying to understand something that wasn't meant for me to understand. When you are like that, it not only affects you but everyone around you.

I know all of this is easier said than done, but it can be done. I am telling you guys when I felt my first heartbreak, I could not breathe, and I felt like my world was over. Trust me, you will be okay, and you will get over it. When I am sick or sad, I fix myself up with a nice outfit, makeup and my hair done. When you look pretty, you feel better. If you are sitting around the house looking a mess, you are going to feel a mess. Go out with your friends, spend time with your family, or try a new activity. Do anything but sit in the house, even when you do not want to get out of the house. Remember everything happens for a reason, and God doesn't make any mistakes. Even when you are at your lowest, know that with God anything is possible.

"Trust in the LORD with all your heart and lean not on your understanding; in all your ways submit to him, and he will make your paths straight." Proverbs 3: 5-6

Activity *17*
1. Is there something you have been stressed and sad about for a long time?

2. Bounce back and get out of the slump. Stressing won't make it better, but getting up and moving will.

Day 18

Worry about Yourself

When I started my business and even more so when I started writing this book I found so many people worrying about me. Not out of concern but plain old nosey. It was so apparent that I had to step back and take a look at myself to make sure I wasn't one of those people. One of the worst things you can waste your time on is worrying about other people's business. Are you that person, who is always on the outside looking into someone else's life? Are you that person that is envious of someone else's life? If you were honest with yourself and answered yes, you have to stop that now. I think we have all been at that place at some level in our lives. So many people work so hard and struggle because they are trying to compete with someone else when you should be worrying about yourself. Society makes you think; you should look a certain way, drive a certain car, or live in a big house, and because of that many people are constantly trying to live up to certain expectations. You cannot worry about what kind of car your friend is driving or the kind of house they reside in. In some situations from the outside looking in, they are looking good, but inside they are struggling to make that car and house payment. In the back of your mind, you are wondering what are they doing so different? Especially if you know them well, and you may have an idea about their income. Stop praising material things, because it can be taken away at any moment. I have had friends in the past that would spend hours a day obsessing over someone and what they had. They would try and get the same designer bags, clothes, hairstylist, and anything else they could get, knowing they were living a life they could not afford, just to impress people who were not giving them any thought. I have had my share of envious moments in my life, but I am too parsimonious to try and keep up with someone with material things.

    I had a friend who was disrespectful and rude, but it seemed like God was always blessing her. I know that sounds crazy, but I was so envious of her. She was very selfish and mean to her mother, but just moved from one nice townhouse to this massive brick house in a great neighborhood. I would always wonder how someone so hateful could continue to be so blessed, and here I was still in my two bedroom apartment wishing that I could afford to live in a big house like that. One day while visiting my friend's house I noticed as she got dressed she had left the tag on her shirt. I discretely told her that the tag was on her shirt. She said, "Girl, I know I am going to take it back tomorrow." I was so shocked when she did that because I never thought about going to purchase a shirt with money I needed, to later return it to replace the money I spent. She would always say, "Girl you do what you have to do when you have kids to feed." We were close for many years, and I became close with her mother, and we would often talk. During this time, her mother had just got a job, and she was complaining about how her daughter was trying to take all of her checks. I was trying to make the situation better, and I said well maybe she needs it to pay rent or bills. The mother said, "She doesn't need that much money, Section 8 pays the majority of her rent." That moment there, I realized you can't be worrying about what someone is doing or what they have. Here I was on the outside looking in trying to figure out how she was able to afford the new clothes and the fancy house. When in reality she was purchasing some of those clothes and returning them the next day, and living in a $1,600 a month house only paying $400 a month. I had wasted all of that time worrying about her false life when I could have been improving mine.

So, when you are worrying about someone else, stop and continue to worry about yourself. People use to swear I had a perfect relationship because we would always take good pictures and post them on social media, not knowing we were going through some tough times. If you worry about yourself and stop seeking validation from others, stop trying to compete and being envious of others, you will see that you will become a happier person. Put all of the time and energy you use worrying about others into bettering yourself, and you will see your life change before your eyes.

Activity 18
1. Is there anybody or anything that you obsess over (always looking at their social media, and always talking about them, jealous of material possessions?)
2. Can you recall a time in your life, where you have been envious or jealous of someone? How did you handle it and get over it?

Day 19

Spend Time with the People You Love

Sometimes life can be so overwhelming, that we forget about the important things in life. We are so focused on things that are unimportant that we take life for granted. How often do you spend time with people who truly love and support you? How many times do you show appreciation to people who support you? So many times we waste time trying to fight to be in others' lives when they do not make the same effort to be in ours. I know that I have given so much time and energy to people who did not deserve it. I always mention the time when I was talking to my friend Juice, and he asked if I had talked to some of our mutual friends, and I went to tell him no, and how it hurt my feelings that no one had reached out to me. He told me not to worry about the people that were not there but worry about the people that were there. Once he said that it had given me a reality check. I had so many people who loved me and cared for me who showed me often, but yet my feelings were hurt because other's that I felt should care didn't.

"People inspire you, or they drain you – pick them wisely." ~Hans F Hansen

"Surround yourself with only people who are going to lift you higher." ~Oprah Winfrey

"Keep away from people who try to belittle your ambitions. Small people always do that, but the really great make you feel that you too, can become great. When you are seeking to bring big plans to fruition, it is important with whom you regularly associate. Hang out with friends who are like-minded and who are also designing purpose-filled lives. Similarly, be that kind of a friend for your friends." ~Mark Twain

In this crazy world we live in, it is very important for us to surround ourselves with positive people. Life is so short, and you never know when a person will take their last breath. Back in 2003, I moved to Albany, Georgia away from all of my family but my mama. When I first left, I would visit almost every weekend, and I would visit my grandmother and spend the night with her. As time passed, and she moved back to her hometown Summerville, Ga, which is probably 30 minutes away from Rome, I did not see her as much as I should when I visited. I took her and that time for granted. My grandmother was my biggest supporter, and it wasn't anything that she wouldn't have done for me. I have my moments where I miss her, and I think back to all of the times that I could have visited and I didn't. So it is important for so many reasons why you should spend time with the people you love. I felt like after a while I was going home just to go to funerals. Spend time with the people you love because you can never get those precious moments back.

Activity 19
1. When is the last time you went on a family outing?
2. When is the last time you called your main supporters to tell them, you love and appreciate them?

Pull your calendar out and plan a day for you and your family. Plan something that is inexpensive, that everyone could join. Start calling your family members for suggestions, and give them your ideas, so they will feel like they are a part of it. Start living and make good memories with your family and stop taking people for granted.

Day 20

Don't be insecure

Being insecure is one of the worst characteristics to have, and it's a characteristic that many of us deal with on a daily basis. It's one of those thorns that is so hard to pick. The truth of the matter is, we may be dealing with more than one insecurity at a given time. It could be the complexion of your skin, the shape of your body and so much more. My mama used to call me all of the time and ask me what I was doing, and my answer would always be, I am just thinking. She would always respond by saying you think too much. Thinking a lot can be beneficial and unhealthy at the same time it just depends on how you use it. I was always thinking of a plan for success, but at the same time, I was dissecting my life too much. I would just always think of the bad things that were impending in my life instead of counting my blessings. Focusing only on the negative things would make me feel bad because I hadn't reached the level of understanding. I didn't quite understand why it was taking me so long to get to the level of success I desired. I wasn't looking at everything I had accomplished, only what I did not accomplish. Negative self-talk is a one-way ticket on the path of self-destruction and will contribute significantly to your insecurities. I had to own my flaws and accept my imperfections, and work on the things I could change realizing that we are imperfect people trying to be perfect in an imperfect world.

Growing up I never attributed the issues that I dealt with came from insecurities. At that time, I, at least, didn't acknowledge that was the root of certain behaviors I attained as a young girl. I didn't know why I was extra sensitive or always had a bad attitude. 2009 was the year; it was apparent that I had insecurities because it was taking over my life in a negative way. When I was in a wheelchair, I didn't want to come out of the house, because I always felt like people were staring at me. The weight gain was a big contribution to my insecurities. I knew that I couldn't live in self-pity, and I had to work on my self-esteem. I hated the way I looked and the weight I had gained, and I became so insecure that I did not even like to take pictures anymore, and I always thought I was photogenic. I knew that I had to do something to change the way that I was feeling, and start being happy again. I relished the fact that I wanted to be in a happy place. I couldn't afford physical therapy, so I would practice standing a few seconds, and practiced walking until I learned how to do it. Once I learned how to walk, I started working on my weight. It did not make any sense to keep complaining about something if I wasn't going to try and fix the problem. I understood that to rid myself of my insecurities and to find true happiness it started with me.

When you learn that your true happiness comes from within, and no certain person has the power to make you happy, you have won most of the battle. True happiness cannot come from how others make you feel; they can only enhance the happiness that you have already obtained. How you feel about yourself determines so much in your life. If you are happy and confident with yourself, you feel like you can conquer every goal that you write down. If you are unhappy with self-esteem issues, it is hard for you to go into something with the confidence you need. Initially, you have to accept your flaws and imperfections, and know that God created you in his own image, and you are beautiful just the way you are. Overcoming your insecurities will not happen overnight, but if you work towards them diligently, it will happen. You must change your perception of happiness. Are you looking for happiness to come from instant gratification or are you looking for an internal happiness that gives you peace of mind? Remember your accomplishments, and practice positive self-talk with positive affirmations. We have already covered your fears, doubts and more, so now it should be easier to identify where your insecurities come from so you can start working on them. Remember we are in control of our happiness and have the power to change the things we do not like. If you can wake up and be positive in spite of the situation, then you are on the right track to finding a place if true happiness.

Activity 20
1. List at least two things that make you are insecure.
2. What are two ways that you can work on improving your insecurities today?

If we are insecure about things we can change, we need to work hard for that change. If you are insecure about things you can't change, pray for strength and wisdom to know how to deal with it.

Day 21

Break the Habit

Have you ever heard the old myth, "It takes 21 Days to Form a Habit" by Maxwell Maltz? Studies have shown that it takes around 21 Days to form a new habit, and newer studies have shown after 66 days the habit will start to form. So congratulate yourselves on your 21 Days of positivity thus far. You have gone 21 Days straight on bettering yourself, and since you have been consistent, it hardly profits to backtrack now. From this day forward, make a conscious decision to be happy and speak nothing but positivity in your life. If a situation or a person does not benefit you, then you need to remove yourself. From this day forward you need to choose to have the life you want. In the last 21 Days, you have revealed some of your deepest inner feelings, and you have learned the things that cause negativity in your life. You have won most of the battle. Now, it is up to you to use every mistake and failure as a learning opportunity to make your life great. You have decided that you must hold yourself accountable and allow the healing process to begin soothing all of the hurt and pained you have endured in the past. To soar in this new skin, make new memories and accomplish new goals. Allow God to use you, and walk in your purpose and live the life he planned for you. However with forming these new habits you should use the same principal to break the old habits. For example, if watching tv is taking up a considerable amount of time then turn the tv off at 6 pm for 21 days. Yes, I know all the reality shows come on at 8. Certain things we do are so second nature that we don't see it as a bad habit. If you call your best friend to talk about the other best friend, then try to eliminate negative conversation for 21 days that indecisively will manifest 21 days of positive conversation.

After I had started my healing my process, I began to start feeling better about myself. Incidentally, I was enlightened on the weight that lifted off my shoulders. I knew that everything would take time, but as long as I continued to pray, had faith and believed, I would live a happy, successful life. I knew that I was tired of living my life trying to please and make other people happy. I was ready to make a change, and I was grateful to have another chance to make it right. I continued to repeat my positive affirmations daily, and I started to believe everything that I said. When I moved back to Atlanta in March 2015, I was ready to face my demons and confront everything that hurt me. I was ready to forgive myself and others for the past and move on and truly find happiness. I had been through so much in the last seven years, and my confidence, self-esteem, and life had taken me on an emotional rollercoaster. My foundation started with God, and I knew that I could get through anything if I kept the faith and continued to believe in God's word. I was ready to break the habit, and form new positive habits and speak it into existence.

After I had started forming new habits, my life changed. If I woke up with an attitude or in a bad mood, I immediately thanked God for waking me up, and I started praying. I had to first start with my attitude because I was aware that with a positive attitude, I would have a positive outcome and negative energy only breeds negative energy. I started applying this in every situation, and I was determined not to go back to my old ways. I took everything that I learned and used it for the good. I didn't worry about things that I couldn't control, and I lived one day at a time. I stopped worry about the past and future and started living in the present. I started working harder than ever, but because I was walking in my purpose, it did not feel like work. I was preparing myself to have a great life. I already knew that I would face challenges, and just because I wanted to change didn't mean that life would stop. I knew that I would still face tough decisions and situations, but it was the way I reacted that would determine the outcome. I was going into 2016 with new habits, and leaving all of the bad habits in 2015. I knew that my life was good, and I was blessed, but I was ready to be great.

Activity 21
Remember we are in control of our lives. So let's break the habit of having negativity hinder you from being the best you.

Day 22

New Season of Increase

"Nothing can stop the man with the right mental attitude from achieving his goal, nothing on earth can help the man with the wrong attitude." ~Thomas Jefferson

"When I started counting my blessings, my whole life turned around." ~Willie Nelson

    We have already established that with having the right attitude and God, anything is possible. You have to speak the life you want into existence. Now, that you have left the past in the past, and you have prayed and made your vision plain, you can see clearly. Your vision is clear, and you know what you need to do to become a better person and have the life you always wanted. Once you have learned to be grateful and be thankful for what you have, God will bless you with more. Growing up, if a big opportunity came your way, my family would tell you to claim it and say if it was meant to be, God would give you everything you need. After I had made it through my paralysis, I knew that God had bigger plans for me. When we go through things in life, we are going through the test, and later on, those tests become our testimonies. Everything we go through in life good or bad is only preparing us for what God has planned for us. All of the trials and tribulations that we go through are meant to make us stronger and wiser. I also had to realize that as long as I was going through I was not stuck. I decided that I needed to decrease so that God could increase in my life. Shed some junk out of my trunk and make room for the many blessings God had wanted me to have. It is true God won't bless a bunch of mess. He is waiting to bless you abundantly. For that to happen, we have to allow God to be God. One thing I had to realize is that I needed him more than he needed me. I needed all that he had to offer. Simply make it your season for the increase.

In May of 2015, I was laid off from my job, and I felt it was a sign for me to focus on my own business. I knew that it would be a big sacrifice not to look for another job, but I was determined to go for my dreams. I claimed everything in advance. I truly believed that God would bless me and that financially I would be okay. After I had been laid off, I started to host different boot camps and fitness contest. I had no idea, how I was going to pay for anything that I was doing. I had also started working on a fitness t-shirt line and my first book. All of my money went to bills and my son, and I did not have any money left over to invest. Even though my money was low, I still had faith and believed everything would work out, and I claimed it. I was able to host the boot camps, fitness contest, photo shoots and more because God provided for me. When I first started writing this book, I knew publishing the book and marketing the book was not in my budget, but I didn't worry about that. I had already claimed success for my book, so all I felt like I had to do was finish and do the needed research and God would show up and show out like he always did. So if you are reading this book, then you know God came in and showed out again.

"I will send you rain in its season, and the ground will yield its crops and the trees their fruit."

~Leviticus 26:4

"If you believe, you will receive whatever you ask for in prayer. ~Matthew 21:22

So, in this new season in 2016 claim it and know

that this is your season for increase and nothing can stand in the way of that but you. We have broken our old habits, and we will no longer allow doubt, fear and negativity stand in the way of our blessings. Do not allow money or people to discourage you from your dreams. As I was writing this book, I did not have the money to publish it, but I knew if I did my part God would meet me more than halfway. If I got the product and put 100 percent in, God would meet me more than half, and bless me with more than I ever imagined. 2016 is your season of increase and to be great, so be great and always work on being a better you. 2016 will be the year that you are successful or reach higher goals.

Activity 22
What is something that you want to happen this year? I want you to work hard and claim it. Remember if you put forth 100 percent and have faith, God will meet you more than halfway.

Day 23

Give Back

"No act of kindness, however small, is ever wasted"
~Aesop

I know growing up, you have always heard it is better to give than receive. So many times, we get caught up with our wants and needs, we forget to give back to others. Giving back could be anything from feeding the homeless, providing clothes, or providing free services to help people that are less fortunate. Giving back not only help others but it also helps build confidence. Helping others has always lifted my spirit, no matter the situation that I was going through. If I was feeling downhearted, or feeling like I had no purpose, helping others would make me feel better about myself. I felt like I had a purpose and there is no better feeling than seeing the smile on other's faces. I remember when I volunteered to help donate food, clothes, and personal items to the homeless, I left feeling like I made a difference. It gave me a reality check on how blessed I was. I have found myself complaining about simple things or not having something I wanted when there were people that were living outside. The feeling that I had to help was unexplainable, and this is something I knew that I wanted to do forever.

In 2013, when I started my business, everyone would ask me why my prices were so low. I always felt that the most important thing was to help others. I truly felt that if I helped God would supply me with all of my needs. I would work all day long without getting tired because I loved what I was doing. As my business grew, I knew I had to raise my prices so that I could keep my business going, but I still wanted to help women that were less fortunate. I started hosting free to only a $5 charge for virtual challenges providing women with all of the tools they needed to be successful in their weight loss journey. I would also do a free one on one personal training sessions with women or charge them half price if they were going through financial difficulties. I felt God had blessed me to a blessing to others, and I was receiving all of the blessings I asked for and more. Sometimes we have to think about the importance of helping others. I think it is in my raising to be a giver the way I am. My mother would always allow people to stay with us when they had nowhere to go. I never understood that and would often get mad when we had to share our space with others. It is funny now, but all of the things that I didn't understand that my mama did back then to help other people, I ended up doing the same thing. I often open my doors when I can help someone in their time of need.

I remember when I first moved to Atlanta, I was amazed at how many homeless people and how many people would walk up to you and your car and ask you for money. I had never seen anything like it before. I never witnessed people sleeping outside, and hungry. We are blessed with so many things that we often take for granted, because we feel we are entitled to everything we have when we are not. That is why it is so important to remain humble and help others because you never know if one day your life will have a drastic change. You have to think of a time when you were going through a tough time in your life, and you needed someone. Always treat people the way you would want them to treat you. People would always tell me not to give money to the homeless people they were just going to buy drugs with it. It didn't matter to me either way, because I just wanted to do my part, and they would have to deal with the consequences of their actions. So every time I see someone on the side of the road, or if someone comes up to me, and I have extra money, I always give. I am going to always live my life to be a blessing to others because I know that God truly blesses me.

"Give, and it will be given to you. A good measure, pressed down shaken together and running over, will be poured into your lap. For with the measure you use, it will be measured to you." ~Luke 6:38

"Every man shall give as he is able, according to the blessing of the LORD your God which HE has given you" ~Deuteronomy 16:17

Activity 23

Plan a day where you can give back. They're so many ways to give back for example; donate food, clothes and personal items, read to children, and so many other things. Take a moment not to think of yourself, but someone else that is in need, and be a blessing.

Day 24

Have Fun

"Even though you're growing up, you should never stop having fun." ~ Nina Dobrev

"Winning is only half of it. Having fun is the other half." ~Bum Phillips

"Never ever underestimate the importance of having fun." ~Randy Pausch

"If you're not having fun it's not worth doing." ~Tommy Bolin

Who doesn't enjoy hanging out with the ones they love, smiling, laughing and having fun? We all love to have a good time, but how often in life do we get to do something that we enjoy and love doing. Many of us get so consumed with work and family that we do not make the time to go out and enjoy ourselves. I have lived in Atlanta for several years a place I love with so much to see, but I have not made the time to take advantage of the city. Before I had my son, people would always say, especially my mama, "Girl if I was young, looked like you with no kids, I would be out living life." I did not understand what she meant. As far as I was concerned I thought I was ok because I was doing what I wanted to do when and how I wanted to do it. Mostly I was spending a great deal of time thinking about what I could do next to better myself. After becoming a mother, I finally understood what my mother was saying. Now I tell people that do not have kids the same thing because life changes after you have children. When I had my child, my mama would say, "Girl, if I was your age, looked like you, with one kid, I would go out and enjoy myself, because you have a babysitter, and you still need to make time for you." She would even say the baby needs a break from you as well. It took me a minute to adjust to motherhood, but once I did, I knew that it was very important for me to make time for myself. I had been out of the loop for so long that I didn't even get invites anymore, so I didn't know what to do. I was no longer the social butterfly, I used to be, and I needed a welcomed change in my life.

With a little nudging, I started getting out of the house a little at a time. My greatest challenge was trying to find balance. With being a new mother I was tired more and didn't feel like going through the process of getting ready to go out. I started pushing myself to go out, and it made me feel refreshed, I had finally found a balance. I would do whatever I wanted to do at the moment; it could be to get pampered with a manicure and pedicure, go out to eat, or get a drink with a few friends. If I received an invite from someone, I attended the event. I would get my calendar and make sure I planned an outing three to four times a month just for me, and sometimes it was more. Don't get me wrong as a new mother I would feel guilty for going out because here I was again worried about what people thought of me. I felt that it would make me look like an unfit mother. Lord knows after being in the house for a year with a new baby that outlook changed fast and in a hurry. I realized that becoming a mother did not mean that my life had to stop. If I had a bad day or if I was feeling overwhelmed, I would do something that I enjoyed doing, and it would uplift my spirit. It not only lifted my spirits, but it allowed me to give the baby the attention he needed with a fresh approach. Every chance I get, I try to have fun and enjoy my life. In 2014 and 2015 so many young people in my hometown were killed, and it was an eye-opener, that life is too short to be anything but happy. You may have to explore and be adventurous in finding new activities with friends or alone. Just make sure you put having a fun day on your priority list.

Activity 24

So I want you to plan a day of fun without your kids, and without your mate, make this day only about you. Think of something that you love doing and that you haven't done in awhile and enjoy yourself. If you are doing something by yourself, go ahead and purchase your ticket, so you will not back out. If you want to plan your day of fun with one of your friends, then call them now and make a day. Remember that you only have one life to live, and you need to live it to the fullest.

Day 25

What they think of you is none of your business

Are you that person that is always worried about what others think and say about you? If so, we have one more thing in common. I have been consumed by the mere thought more than a few times in my life. Before my relationship with God, I would always seek validation from man instead of him. I couldn't even focus on the happy moments because I would be so worried about what others thought of me. Social media had a very big impact both good and bad. I knew that I could not continue to allow what other people thought of me to bombard in the way of me living my truth. I desired to be happy doing something that I love to do and to live the life I wanted to live. The funny thing is when I was younger I didn't care what people said about me even when I was not behaving appropriately. By the time I reached my mid-twenties, it had started to affect me considerably. After I had become paralyzed I was dealing with my new insecurities, and I was very vulnerable, so instinctively it was easy for most comments to affect me. Going through this tumultuous time hindered me from doing so much. I remember one particular instance during a time when I was using a cane. I had to sing at this club, and I was very nervous about walking on stage. I was so worried about thinking if my show would be good because I had to prop up against a chair to sing. Worrying about what other people thought of me was just another cross that I was going to have to bear.

One thing that I had to learn was, you have to do what makes you happy because people are going to talk about you regardless. In 2013 when I first started my business, I was excited to hear all of the positive feedback in my hometown. I wanted to go back to my hometown to start my business there. I remember I had posted on my Facebook page, that I would be coming home. It was so much positivity coming my way, and then the negativity started coming next. In my hometown, I was known for singing, and overcoming my paralysis. I had evolved past those accomplishments and became a motivational speaker and a personal trainer. However the growth, there were those that doubted me. I remember I was talking to one my ex-boyfriends, and he said, "Yeah everybody saying if Meisha can train you anybody can." My first reaction was, why would he tell me that, and who said it. Did they not believe in me, did they think that I wasn't capable because of my handicap? That comment affected me and added to my insecurities. Here I was happy that I had fought my way past being paralyzed and lost all of the weight I had gained. I wanted to share my newfound knowledge and help other people. They didn't understand this was not a fluke. I attended school to become an elite personal trainer. So, therefore, I had the education and the expertise. I just didn't understand how people could be so crude with their negative remarks. I should have used that as motivation to go to my hometown and prove them wrong, but instead, I allowed the negativity to out shadow my dream and goal. I let what others thought about me keep me from accomplishing my goals. For a while that bothered me when I was trying to move forward, because I felt defeated. One day I was talking to a friend about my business, and she brought it to my attention that I should do a boot camp in Rome, Georgia, I knew it was time to conquer that fear. In July 2015, I held my first 6-week boot camp challenge, and it was a success. I was able to pick a winner and do a photo shoot with all of the fitness boot camp members. This accomplishment was the most gratifying feeling in the world. Something I was scared to do because of what someone said ended up being something that turned out successful.

My experiences on worrying about what others say about me taught me that, what others think of me is none of my business. If you know who you are, you should not care about what others think. If you know you are beautiful, talented, genuine and a successful person, never let anyone make you feel different. Never dim your light for someone else, always shine. When you stop seeking validation from man and only God, there is no way you will be disappointed.

"For am I now seeking the approval of man, or of God? Or am I trying to please man? If I were still trying to please man, I would not be a servant of Christ."

~Galatians 1:10

"But just as we have been approved by God to be entrusted with the gospel, so we speak, not to please man, but to please God who tests our hearts."
~Thessalonians 2:4

Activity 25
1. Is there something that someone else has said that made you doubt yourself? If yes, how did you fix it?
2. If you are going through this now, pray and ask strength to be delivered from people.
3. Always remember what someone else thinks or says about you is none of your business.

Day 26

Role Model (I look up to you)

Growing up, who did you look up to? Who was your role model when you were younger, and who is your role model now? Who was that person that you admired and wanted to be just like? I wanted to be an R&B superstar, and I wanted to emulate the greats, Patti Labelle, Natalie Cole, Brandy, Aaliyah, Monica. Girl groups like The Supremes, The Emotions, Xscape, TLC, SWV, Destiny's Child and so many more, those were the ones that first came to my mind. Music was my escape and singing was my passion. I wanted to be able to get on stage and have the crowd singing the words to my song, and I wanted to be famous just like them. I would have posters of all of my favorite female and male artist all over my wall. I would dance and sing in the mirror with my hairbrush pretending I was singing in front of a sold out crowd. I would watch BET excessively or listen to my favorite cassette tapes. When I was despondent or feeling melancholy, I would listen to my music, and it would make me feel better no matter what I was going through. Singing was engraved in me, and being trained by my mother at an early age, I knew that was something that I was supposed to do. No matter how many artist I pretended it to be, Monica stood out to me the most, and even now that I am an adult, she is someone I admire.

When Monica came on the scene with her first album, I was around the age 9 or 10, and I fell in love. I would sing "Don't Take it Personal" all around the house, and listen to it over and over again. I remember I sang "For You I will" at a wedding when I was younger, and "Why I love you so Much" and "Before you walk out my life" at talent shows. I was amazed at how strong her voice was at a young age, and I wanted to sing just like her. I will never forget the strength she had when she did her interview on 20/20: The Storm, about her boyfriend killing himself in front of her. We both grew up with our mother's side being "Churchy" and our dad's side being "Street". There were many other artists that I loved, but there was no one that I identified with like Monica. I love the way she showed that in life you may go through challenges and struggles, but it is how you bounce back. Many times you watch people in life be content, but Monica evolved and grew as a woman and a great example of class. She went from being the neck rolling girl with the attitude, to a woman with class taking one day at a time to become a better woman. I could go on and on about Monica, but there is one woman that is my personal role model.

MONICA & MS KAMESHA

Now I do think that it is ok to look at athletes or famous people as role models. I just gave the best example of mine. However, I think sometimes we look so far out that we may not see the role models that are in our presence. Those people who are dear and near to us. My mother Nekolia Isaac is the best example of a strong woman and true role model. She courageously had to endure her struggles, but her greatest struggle was delivering a 6lb 5oz. baby girl who is me three days before her 15th birthday. She overcame all of the statistics and the odds that were thrown her way. No matter the struggles that she endured, she handled them with integrity and class. I definitely would not be the woman that I am today. She is not only my mother but she is my best friend. I have the best of both worlds because I can tell her all of my secrets, but at the same time get the advice I need from a mother's standpoint. She is the reason that I am so driven and goal oriented because she had always believed in me and told me to believe in myself. She is my biggest support system, and I wouldn't trade her for anything in the world.

Activity 26

Who is the person you look up too? Choose someone that shows the best qualities, and qualities you would love to have. I chose women who went through so many struggles but never gave up no matter how tough the situation was. Who is that person for you and why?

Day 27

I love me

"Today you are you, that is truer than true. There is no one alive who is youer than you. ~Dr Suess

Do we know the meaning of love? I would think that everyone may have what they think love is and how it manifests in their particular lives. I feel that love is kind, patient and true. To have these ingredients will be the epitome of self-love. Self-love is the best kind of love to have next to God's love. The unfortunate part about self-love is that many of us take more than half of our lifetime to truly love ourselves. We are subjected to so much of what society idealizes what self-love should be. If you love yourself, then you need to be super skinny. If you love yourself, then you should spend an astronomical amount on your weave. I know you are thinking, I have always loved myself, and that could be true, but I am talking about the self-love you learn when you decide to make the conscious decision to put you first. So many times in our lives we always put the love for others before the love we have for ourselves. We spend most of our lives holding on to friendships and relationships where we give so much love; we subsequently lose ourselves. We put the feelings of others before our feelings, which at times leave us with so much resentment and regret. In this book, we have pondered over many lessons that take us back to a place where we lost our way. The good thing about life is as long as we have breath it's never too late to make the needed changes to have a better life. It is never too late to learn how to love yourself. It is never too late to learn self-worth, and how you really should treat others and how you should be treated as well. Once you love yourself and know your worth, no one has the power to put a value of worth on your life. Of course no matter how much you love yourself, words will hurt, but at the end of the day, you will be able to handle it accordingly. You will never let the negativity that others have for you, change the feeling that you have about yourself. Remember always to be true to yourself.

I have always been raised to believe in myself and love myself. However, I haven't always known how to do that, or truly known my worth. For so long, I would seek validation from people and try to please them. I had expended so much time putting everyone's happiness and feelings before mine that I lost myself in the process. I would participate in activities that I knew that I had no business doing. I participated just to be accepted or make someone else happy. I have been doing that ever since I can remember. I have always been petrified to say no because I would be concerned about people not liking me when in reality the unconditional love of God is all I should have expected. I do not think it was one particular situation that gave me a reality check of the changes that needed to be made. I think once I started holding myself accountable and taking responsibility for my actions, I could then forgive myself and leave the past in the past. I was tired of allowing people to use and abuse me. I was tired of not living up to my full potential, and not living the happy life, I knew I deserved. How could I expect someone else to truly love me and treat me like I needed to be treated if I didn't even love myself enough to respect me? I knew that I had to start setting boundaries, and stay faithful in my word that no matter what God would not let me down.

"Don't ever criticize yourself. Don't go around all day long thinking, 'I'm not as smart as my brother.' God wasn't having a bad day when he made you... If you don't love yourself in the right way, you can't love your neighbor. You can't be as good as you are supposed to be." ~Joel Osteen

"I think every girl needs to love herself, regardless of anything. Like if you're having a bad day, if you don't like your hair, if you don't have the best family situation, whatever, you have to love yourself and you can't do anything until you love yourself first. ~Julianne Hough

"What I am is how I came out. No one's perfect and you just have to accept your flaws and learn to love yourself." ~Kelly Brook

Activity 27
1. What does self-love mean to you?
2. List five things that you love about yourself.

Remember in order to make someone else happy, you have to be happy with yourself first.

Day 28

Today I Commit

I am excited and sad all at the same time that our journey has almost come to an end. We have burrowed very deep into our lives in the last 27 Days. No one expects anyone to heal overnight, but just start the healing process. Take one day at a time and apply positivity in every aspect of your life. You are now aware of your doubts, fears, and insecurities, and that is the first step in the healing process. You have found your purpose and made your vision and goal boards, so now it's time to work. It is time to embrace your uniqueness. There is only one you, and you have only one life to live, so make it count.

When I started my healing process, I started to feel better about myself each day. I knew that I wasn't 100 percent healed, but I knew the effort meant growth. I still make mistakes, but I always try to right my wrongs. I hate having confrontations, and fall outs, and I try to prevent them but sometimes they happen. I have a conscious now, and I feel bad when I lose my cool, and I immediately apologize. I used to be too stubborn to apologize, but feel so bad about the argument and dwell on it for days and days, instead of just doing the adult thing and apologizing. One time I let a friend stay with me for a while which is something that I was hesitant about because living with someone is hard. If you are not real friends, and the respect level is not equal on both parts, it will not work and will destroy whatever relationship you have. One night we were having a normal discussion, which lead to some sensitive topics. I didn't agree with the overbearing judgment, and I didn't think she should have such a strong opinion about my family business. I was becoming more irritated by the conversation. I became very infuriated and started raising my voice. Instead of just ending the conversation, it kept going, and we both started taking jabs at each other. About 30 to 45 minutes after the argument was over, I felt remorseful because I shouldn't have let anything she said affect me to the point that I did not have self-control, so I apologized. The things I said were my truth, but that wasn't the time to say it in a heated argument. I knew that apologizing for my part was the adult thing to do. I didn't care if she forgave me because that was her choice, but I did my part. I knew that I was maturing as a woman and that putting my pride aside and apologizing was a step in the right direction for me. I discussed the situation the next day prayed and asked for forgiveness, and I moved on. I have learned to use every mistake as a learning opportunity, and will continue to make every effort not to allow anyone to have that much control over me that I lose control. I knew that I wanted to be a better person, and I was going to work at it every day.

Activity 28

The day that I prayed to God, and asked him for strength and guidance to walk in my purpose the way that he would want me to, I wrote myself a letter. I wrote a commitment letter to myself, and I put it on my calendar, so I could see it every day. I wanted to read the letter every day until I was committed to being a better me in every aspect of my life. Today I want you to write a commitment letter to yourself. Below is the commitment letter that I wrote to myself.

Dear Meisha,

Today I want to commit to being a better me. No longer will I live in the past, or allow anyone to make me feel bad about my past. Each day I will continue to pray, read my Bible, and walk in my purpose. I am going to embrace the new me with open arms. I am going to smile more, laugh more and live more. I am not going to allow my doubts, fears, insecurities, to get in the way of me accomplishing my goals and dreams. I am going to treat people like I want to be treated, but set boundaries. I am going to be the best mother and woman that I can be. I will not stress over things that I cannot change, and I will live one day at a time. I commit to loving myself and valuing myself. No longer will I allow the way someone else feels about me or what they say or think about me affect me, because I know who I am. I will love me first; I will be successful. ~Meisha

Day 29

Never Give Up

Our journey is about to come to an end, and after everything we have been through in our lives, we know that with God anything is possible. I know life can be very challenging, and at times, it seems like we will not make it through. That is when you need to lean on God for his understanding. I have been through so much in my life, and I can remember times when I did not think I was strong enough to make it through, but I always did. When I sit back and think about my life, there was never a time that God did not bring me through. If I had a plan that did not work, God had a better plan already worked out for me. Giving up is definitely not an option.

There are so many things in my life that I did not complete. My mom always says that I am always all over the place because I am so talented which contributes to me not completing anything. Well, I don't know how true that is but what I do know is that I have given up more times than I would like to admit to but that is officially the old me. So much about me, I have discovered while writing this book. My mom has her opinion, but I realize now I gave up because I was afraid. The older I get, I think about all the time that was wasted because I did give up. One Sunday, my Pastor's sermon topic was, pressing to your blessing. All, in a nutshell, no matter how hard it gets keep pressing your way. I know everyone that is reading this has a story and has been through some things that you did not think that you were going to be able to make it through, but you did. Below are some of my favorite quotes about never giving up.

"Don't quit. Never give up trying to build the world you can see, even if others can't see it. Listen to your drum and your drum only. It's the one that makes the sweetest sound." ~Simon Sinek

"If you really believe in what you're doing, work hard, take nothing personally if something blocks one route, find another one. Never give up. ~Laurie Notaro

"You just never give up, no matter how hard the challenges are, and observe this world with a healthy dose of criticism and don't follow the herd like somebody else might do." ~Renny Harlin

"I will keep smiling, be positive and never give up! I will

give 100 percent each time I play. These are always my goals and my attitude." ~Yani Tseng

Once you have realized that giving up is not an option, and you continue to work hard, there is no way you can lose. When I became paralyzed, and the doctors told me that it was a possibility that I would never walk again, I could have given up then, but I knew that was not an option. I was 25 years old, and I knew that I had a lot of life to live, and I could not take the word of man, but believe that God would bring me through. Once I learned to walk again, I knew that I wasn't finished yet, because I truly felt that God did not bring me through that time in my life not to inspire someone else. I wanted to inspire as many people as I could. I knew that God blessed me to be a blessing to others. I knew that my journey wasn't going to be easy, and I knew that nothing worth having comes easy. I will continue to sacrifice because I believed in God and his word. Writing this book has not been easy there were times I wanted to give up. In the days that the GIVE UP SPIRIT decided to visit I had to go to the word. Below are some of my favorite scriptures that always get me through some of my toughest times.

"I can do all things through him who strengthens me." ~Philippians 4:13

"And let us not grow weary of doing good, for in due season we will reap, if we do not give up." ~Galatians 6:9

"But you, take courage! Do not let your hands be weak, for your work shall be rewarded."

~2 Chronicles 15:7

"Rejoice always, pray without ceasing, give thanks in all circumstances; for this is the will of God in Christ Jesus for you. ~1 Thessalonians 5:16-18

"Ask, and it will be given to you; seek, and you will find; knock, and it will be opened to you. For everyone who asks receives, and the one who seek finds, and to the one who knocks it will be opened."

~Matthew 7:7-8

Day 30

Live your life

Today is the end of our journey together, and if you have completed reading the book this obviously means that you have unambiguously made a conscious decision to work on you, however, it is only the beginning of your journey to a better you. The healing process has started, your fitness journey has started, and there are goals that you have to complete. I am not saying that you will never face another problem again, but it does mean that you are in a better place to control the outcome. I want you to apply everything that we have talked about each day and apply it to your life without second guessing yourself. Live your life one day at a time, without regret. From this day forward you are going to walk in your purpose, and live the life you were destined to have. Please remember that you are in control of your life and your destiny. You have the power to live a happy and successful life whether it is good or bad. We have learned throughout the book, that you cannot allow what man say affect you, and stop you from doing what you feel is best for you. Your time is limited on this earth, so you have to make the best of it. Always follow your heart and your intuition, and never allow what someone else feel about you change what you already know about yourself. You are an heir to the highest and no matter what you are loved. Don't forget the most important relationship that you have is with God. God will intuitively be there no matter the time or the day, no matter the issue. No problem is too big for God. If a day arise and you can't get your mojo back, just reread this book or go to the day that you are struggling with and go back through the exercise. You can do it!

Now that your vision is transparent, and you see the light at the end of the tunnel, why not go all the way to the end? Use all of the doubt and negativity that is thrown your way only for motivation to go harder. Below I am going to give you 21 ways that you can live your life to the fullest.

> 1. Live each day one day at a time, and have a fresh start, and never bring yesterday's trouble in today.

2. Be proactive and never wait for someone to do what you can do. Remember no one is going to work harder for you than you.
3. Always be willing to grow and learn.
4. Set goals and complete them.
5. Never let what man say affect you, always know your worth and who you are.
6. Learn from constructive criticism, and be open-minded.
7. Always turn a negative into a positive.
8. Do not bad mouth or criticize other people, and mind your own business.
9. Only surround yourself with people who will make you better, not bitter.
10. Always give back, and be grateful.
11. Workout and Live a healthy lifestyle.
12. Continue to upgrade yourself.
13. Try new things
14. Live with a conscious
15. Remember the only person you can change is yourself.
16. Embrace change and take risks.
17. Love yourself and always know your self-worth
18. Love others and treat them the way you want to be treated.
19. Never stop learning.
20. Get out there and meet new people.

21. Stop complaining, be true to yourself, live your life and never give up.

I promise if you apply all of those things to your life it will make a drastic change. It doesn't matter how old you are; it is never too late to try again. As long as you have breath, you should always work on being a better you and having a better life. Now, you have the tools to live the life that you are supposed to be living. Just because the 30 days are over does not mean that you stop. Never stop working on you and never stop living your life. Know that this journey is not going to be easy, and every day is not going to be good. You still are going to have bad days, and when the devil see that you are trying to do better, he is going to get busy. I remember during the process of writing this book, the devil was on my back trying to distract me from finishing this book. Many times I would get thrown off, but I was determined to finish, and I wasn't going to let anyone stop me. I knew the life that I wanted, and I was going to get it. I was going to be a better me.

21 Days of Fitness

Okay so now on to us looking better!! You can work out All DAY, but if you don't eat right then, you are working out for nothing. When I did my first 30 Day Challenge, I did good the first couple of weeks, with my eating and I was working with a personal trainer, and I saw results fast, but after that second week, I started going back to fast foods. Keep in mind I would still be working out, but now I didn't see many results. So if you want to see results, then you REALLY have to eat right. You know they say, you are what you eat.

It is not only important to eat right, but drinking water is very important also. Eating healthy is a challenge for many people, but you can do it. When you go grocery shopping, do not go while you are hungry. I read somewhere it is best to eat something before, so your mouth's not making the decisions. Also, plan out meals for the week, that way you will know exactly what to eat, because eating healthy can get very expensive. I plan my meals ahead of time and make my grocery list. When I do not have a list, I always go over my budget

SHOPPING HEALTHY

When you are shopping, make sure you pick fresh vegetables and fruits and watch the ripeness, because you want them to last through the week. When you shop, think about how much fruit a day you will be eating. You can eat a variety of fruit: fresh, frozen, canned, or dried. Eat more dark green veggies: broccoli, and other leafy greens; orange veggies such as carrots, sweet potatoes. Also, eat beans and peas: pinto beans and kidney beans, black beans and split peas. When you are getting dairy products get low-fat cheeses, and non-fat or 1% milk and yogurt. Look for lean cuts of beef and pork that says loin or round. Make sure you bake or grill your meat, and do not FRY!! Try and stay away from all whites; bread, white rice, white flour, sugar, and potatoes, and salt. Look for whole grain products. Also, look on the back of the label readings. You can keep track of the servings, calories, total fat, etc.

I buy frozen fruits instead of a lot of fresh fruits. Of Course, I buy oranges, bananas, and I freeze my grapes. I separate them in containers and eat them for snacks throughout the day. Strawberries are my favorite fruit for smoothies, so I buy frozen strawberries, and they last a lot longer. I also buy frozen blueberries, blackberries, peaches, mixed fruit, and raspberries. Buying frozen is cheaper and it last longer than fresh fruit. Drink LOTS of water and stay away from sodas, you have already conquered 70% of the battle. Eating healthy is more important than working out. When you get the urge to eat unhealthy, just think about that hard workout you just completed. In a McDonald's meal, you eat 1,000 calories, but only burn maybe 500-700 calories in one workout, and that is working out hard. In my meal plan, I give you so many options on healthy things to eat. Don't be afraid to try new things. Trust me, you can learn to eat healthily and enjoy it.

Okay so in my experience with assisting my clients with their weight loss journey, everyone likes to eat different things. Some people love smoothies in the morning and others may not. I am still amazed at how many grown people tell me they don't eat vegetables and beans. I mean there is no way around eating vegetables, you just have to find vegetables you like. With healthy eating, you have to do what works best for you, what someone else does, may not work for you. My mama can juice and enjoy it, but I can't juice and enjoy it. I would rather eat healthy solid foods, than just juice. Everything is mental, and if you find something you like, it will be easier for you to continue and become successful on your weight loss journey. So it would be a waste of time for me to make up this nice meal plan with food you may or may not like. Below I have a list of healthier choices for you to choose. Remember try to fix smaller portions, or leave food on your plate. You can do this; it is mental, and you have to reprogram your mind because you can love healthy eating too.

Eating Healthy on a Budget (Meal Plan)

Just like most of you, I have fallen off so many times with healthy eating, because my money was low. I would go to the grocery store and spend over my grocery budget buying healthy foods that went to waste. I would buy lots of fruits and vegetables, and they would go bad by the time I tried to cook them. I did not have the money to buy more food, so then I would just eat whatever I had in the house. After many times of overspending, I knew that I had to find a way a way to save money while still eating healthy. I started making weekly menus, and I would buy only what I needed. So to make things a lot easier for you, I have provided 13 breakfast ideas, 18 lunch/dinner ideas, and 21 snack ideas. I have provided a list of better and healthier choices for you to choose. Eating healthy does not have to be a bad thing, and it is something that you can learn to love. Remember it is all mental.

Breakfast

I know you have heard that breakfast is the most

important meal, and that statement is so true. You should eat within two hours of waking up. If you do not eat breakfast, that is like you trying to drive your car on empty. It is important to get all of the nutrients, you need to fuel your day.

Instead of Eating This	Eat This
Bacon	Turkey Bacon
Sausage	Turkey Sausage
Whole Milk/2% Milk	Non-fat/1%/Almond Milk
Yogurt w/ milk	Non-fat/low-fat yogurt
Cheese	Low-fat cheese
Biscuits/White Bread	Low-fat whole grain breads and rolls
Sugar Cereal/Granola	Whole grain, oatmeal, low-fat granola,
Eggs (2 eggs a day won't hurt)	Egg Whites
Donuts	English muffins

Lunch & Dinner

I know that breakfast is very important, but what you eat for your lunch and dinner, matters too. You cannot eat fried foods, besides stir fry with olive oil. Baking, broiling, and grilling is the best and safest way to go.

Instead of Eating This	Eat This
Salad dressing	Nonfat/ light salad dressing
Mayonnaise	Nonfat or light mayonnaise
White pasta & White Rice	Whole wheat pasta & brown or wild rice
All-purpose white flour	Whole-wheat flour
Americana, blue, cheddar, Colby	Low-fat cheese
Ground beef	Ground Turkey
Hot dogs	Turkey Links, Fat-free hot dogs
Seafood with butter	Seafood cooked w/ olive oil

Snacks

Instead of Eating This	Eat This
Regular Ice Cream	Non-fat or low-fat ice cream or sherbet
Popsicle	Sugar-Free Popsicle
Potato chips and buttered popcorn	Unbuttered, reduced-fat popcorn

Meal Plan Options

Breakfast

#1 Egg Whites, Turkey Bacon, Strawberries
#2 Spinach & Strawberry Smoothie
#3 Oatmeal & Fruit
#4 Whole Grain Cereal with Non-fat/1%/Almond Milk
#5 Meal replacement shakes
#6 Breakfast Burrito with Whole wheat tortilla, egg whites & turkey sausage, vegetables
#7 Egg Whites, Turkey Sausage,
#8 Breakfast Omelet w/ vegetables, and turkey bacon
#9 Banana pancakes w/ strawberries
#10 Low-fat granola parfaits
#11 Egg white muffins w/ fruit
#12 Egg and Turkey Bacon sandwich with whole wheat bread.
#13 2 Boiled eggs w/fruit

(These are just healthy breakfast ideas. You can pick and choose what you want to eat. Remember proportion control, and do not overeat. Drink lots of Water.

30 Days to a Better Me

Lunch / Dinner

#1 Grilled Chicken Salad
#2 Veggie chili
#3 Baked Chicken, asparagus, and pinto beans
#4 Turkey Meatloaf, mashed cauliflower, and green beans
#5 Chicken wings, red potatoes, and beans
#6 Chicken Stir Fry w/ brown rice and vegetables
#7 Shrimp Stir Fry w/ brown rice and vegetables
#8 Black bean & brown rice and sauté vegetables
#9 Spaghetti with Whole wheat and ground turkey & mushrooms
#10 Grilled Chicken with broccoli and brown rice
#11 Turkey Vegetable Soup (Ground Turkey
#12 Low-fat Lasagna (Brown Pasta, Ground Turkey
#13 Turkey necks, collard greens, beans
#14 Stuffed Peppers with Brown Rice
#15 Salmon w/ asparagus
#16 Salmon and salad
#17 Baked Fish & Vegetables
#18 Cauliflower Pizza

30 Days to a Better Me

Snacks
#1 Yogurt & Fruit
#2 Fruit Smoothie
#3 Fruit cups
#4 Popcorn
#5 Fruit cups
#6 Peanut butter (natural) with apple slices
#7 Frozen yogurt covered grapes
#8 Apple Slices with Honey
#9 Boiled Eggs
#10 Grapefruit with Honey
#11 Chocolate covered banana popsicles
#12 Chocolate covered banana bites with peanut butter
#13 #Baked sweet potato chips
#14 Frozen yogurt and fruit popsicles
#15 Frozen grapes
#16 Sugar-free jello with fruit cocktail (mixed when prepared)
#17 Banana Pudding (Sugar-free)
#18 Cauliflower Wings
#19 whole wheat fruit quesadilla with strawberries and peanut butter
#20 Frozen fruit & yogurt bites
#21 Cucumber, Tomato Salad

Budget Friendly

Okay, now I know some of you may be reading this thinking where is the healthy eating on a budget part. Now, this is my logic, if you are on a budget, you cannot be too picky about what you are eating. I know there are some people out there who do not like eating the same thing twice in a week, and then they're others like myself, which do not mind. So eating healthy on a budget is for everyone like me. If you are one of those picky eaters, this section may not be for you.

Each week I make a menu of what I will be eating before I go to the grocery store, and I buy what is on the list. I meal prep my meals for three to five days, and I eat meals more than once. Below is an example of my weekly menu for three days and grocery list. If you are new to meal prepping, start off small and only prep for three days. Remember never go to the grocery store hungry, and look in your cabinets to see what you already have, so you will not buy the same thing twice.

Monday	Tuesday	Wednesday
Breakfast Turkey bacon, egg whites, fruit	Breakfast Smoothie	Breakfast Egg White Omelets w/ Tukey bacon
Lunch Chicken Salad	Lunch Chicken Stir Fry w/ brown rice	Lunch Turkey Meatloaf broccoli mashed cauliflower
Dinner Turkey Meatloaf broccoli mashed cauliflower	Dinner Spaghetti and Salad	Dinner Chicken Salad
Snacks Yogurt fruit Popcorn	Snacks Popcorn Yogurt fruit	Snacks Yogurt fruit cup Popcorn

If you have leftovers, put the food in containers and freeze them and keep them for a later day.

(NEVER WASTE FOOD)

Grocery List

Frozen fruit – (Smoothie)

Turkey bacon

Egg whites

Boneless chicken breast – (Chicken Salad, Chicken Stir-fry)

Broccoli

Cauliflower (mashed cauliflower)

Ground Turkey (Turkey Meatloaf, Spaghetti)

Spinach (Salad, Smoothie)

Bell Pepper (Cut up for Stir Fry, Turkey meatloaf, and omelet)

Whole wheat pasta

Oatmeal

Strawberries

Grapes

Bananas

Yogurt

Mrs Dash

Olive Oil

Popcorn

During this time of your healthy eating, Google and Pinterest need to be your best friend. You can search for recipes on Google and Pinterest. Remember to buy what you need, and try to find meals where you are using the same ingredients. Also, when making your menu for the next week, use all of the unused food that you didn't use the previous week. Never waste food, and if you need ideas for different recipes, put the food you want to cook in Pinterest or Google. Remember to eat every two to three hours, three meals and two snacks. Drink the minimum of 64 ounces a day with a goal of a gallon a day or close. This journey is not going to be easy, but it will be worth it.

Workout Plan Tips

Warm up: It is very important to warm up before each workout. Warm up 5 to 10 minutes prior to beginning a resistance training program. Warm muscles perform better!!

LIGHT STRETCH BEFORE YOUR WORKOUT AND DEEP STRETCH AFTER WORKOUT

Make sure you are NOT HOLDING YOUR BREATH (Valsalva maneuver) when you are working out!!

Exhale during the exertion phase
Varied Inhalation/Exhalation during exertion movements

Drink Water, Drink Water, Drink Water, Drink Water, Drink Water

Use the "Recommended Daily Water Intake" from the meal plan guide to get your daily intake need.

Start with the following drinking schedule guide for exercising.

Two hours before	Drink 2 cups of fluid ahead of time

Within 30 minutes before	Drink 1-2 cups prior to starting
Every 10 to 15 minutes during	<u>Drink 6-8 ounces</u>
Within 30 min after	Drink 8 ounces

EAT 2 HOURS BEFORE Workout!! DO NOT WORKOUT ON A FULL STOMACH!! EAT/DRINK PROTEIN AFTER EACH WORKOUT!!

CARDIO EXERCISE (2-3 TIMES A WEEK) + TRAINING PROGRAM

1. 30 MINUTE RUN
2. 30 MINUTES ON TREADMILL/EXERCISING BIKE
3. 30-45 MINUTES SWIMMING
4. 30 MINUTE HIKE/CYCLING

REMEMBER TO EAT CLEAN, EAT CLEAN, EAT CLEAN

IT IS VERY IMPORTANT TO TAKE A BEFORE & AFTER PICTURE! TAKE ONE ON THE 9TH DAY AND THE 30TH DAY... I WOULD LOVE TO SEE YOUR RESULTS AND TESTIMONY... PLEASE SEND TO MSKAMESHA1@GMAIL.COM.... OR Hashtag #MsKamesha #30DaysToaBetterMe

WEEK 1
MONDAY/WEDNESDAY/FRIDAY
30 SEC WALL SIT 1 - 2 SETS OF 15 REPS
(ADVANCE USE WEIGHTS)
GOAL IS 2 SETS

TUESDAY/THURSDAY
30 SECOND EACH/30 SECOND REST

30 MINUTE CARDIO

WEEK 2

MONDAY/WEDNESDAY/FRIDAY
1 MINUTE WALL SIT 2-3 SETS OF 15 REPS
(ADVANCE USE WEIGHTS)
GOAL IS 3 SETS

TUESDAY/THURSDAY
1 MINUTE EACH 30 SEC REST

45 MINUTE CARDIO

WEEK 3
MONDAY/WEDNESDAY/FRIDAY
1 MINUTE WALL SIT 2-3 SETS OF 15 REPS
(ADVANCE USE WEIGHTS)
GOAL IS 3 SETS

TUESDAY/THURSDAY
1 MINUTE EACH 30 SEC REST

45 MINUTE CARDIO

(Butt burner: Starting position... pulse up 15 times... starting position... fire hydrant (lift leg to the side 15 times... starting position... tap 15 times)

No breaks in between

30 Days to a Better Me

CURRENT & PAST CLIENT BEFORE & AFTER PICTURES

Conclusion

In today's society, there are people who practice hate daily. So many times we turn on the news, and see so many senseless deaths. So many innocent people from young to old who are getting murdered because they were at the wrong place at the wrong time. It saddens me to know, that the world is so cruel, and you can take your last breath at any minute. It makes me realize that life is too short not to be happy. Every day that you wake up, you should feel blessed to be alive and make the best of your day. I pray that in reading *30 Days to a Better Me,* you will start the healing process, and choose to put you first.

Remember that you can get through anything, and God will not put more on you than you can handle. Read his word and believe that no matter what you are going through, you will get through it. When times get tough, and you feel like giving up, read this book again. If you are stressed out, read the days that talk about stress and bouncing back. If you are scared to start or finish something because of fear, read the day on doubt and fear. Continue to read your positive affirmations, and complete your goals. You are in control of your life, and with God anything is possible.

Keep in Touch

First I want to thank you so much for purchasing my book *30 Days to A Better Me*. I would love to hear your feedback on what you thought about the book. I would also love to hear your testimonies and see your results. You can send your feedback, testimonies, and results to mskamesha1@gmail.com. I will try my best to answer all emails promptly. Also, follow me on social media, I will talk back to you. I appreciate you just as much as you appreciate me. Talk to You Soon!

www.mskamesha.com

Social media: Twitter,

Facebook, Periscope, YouTube, Instagram, Google – Search "Ms Kamesha"

About the Author

Kamesha "Ms Kamesha" Shropshire always had dreams of becoming successful. However, it wasn't until 2015, when Ms Kamesha decided to put her story to paper, to help inspire others. Ms Kamesha had dreams of becoming an R&B superstar until she was diagnosed with Guillain-Barre Syndrome, and was left paralyzed from the waist down, losing all mobility. Her dreams of becoming a famous singer and dancer were shattered. Doctors told her that there was a chance that she would not be able to walk again or have children. Ms Kamesha never gave up hope and knew that science would only go so far before God stepped in. She began to focus on all of the things she could do, instead of the things she could not do. After learning to walk again, Ms Kamesha was inspired and wanted to help others as she was helped. Ms Kamesha started going to school and became a certified personal trainer, and started her own fitness business. In 2016, Ms Kamesha is going back to her roots and using her voice to inspire others with her new single "A Better Me" to go with her new self-help book "30 Days to a Better Me". She plans to travel to different places motivating and inspiring others to never give up, and be the example and show that with hard work and having a little faith, anything is possible.

"I know that I was put on this earth to inspire the world. I made it through what doctors thought was impossible. God didn't give me the strength to get through all of that just to sit at home and watch TV. He chose me because he knew I was strong enough to get through it, and I would motivate and inspire others. This is what I am meant to do; I am a motivator."

www.mskamesha.com

Social media: Twitter/Facebook/Periscope/YouTube/Instagram/Pinterest - Search "Ms Kamesha"

30 Days to a Better Me

www.ingramcontent.com/pod-product-compliance
Lightning Source LLC
Chambersburg PA
CBHW060537100426
42743CB00009B/1550